High Seas

High Seas

The Naval Passage
to an
Uncharted World

Admiral William A. Owens,
U.S. NAVY

NAVAL INSTITUTE PRESS   ANNAPOLIS, MARYLAND

Library of Congress Cataloging-in-Publication Data
Owens, Williams A., 1940–
  High seas: the naval passage to an uncharted world / William A. Owens.
    p.   cm.
  Includes bibliographical references (p.) and index.
  ISBN 1-55750-661-2 (alk. paper)
    1. United States. Navy—History—20th century. 2. Sea-power—United States.
  3. United States. Navy—Operational readiness. 4. United States—Armed Forces.
  5. United States—Military policy.
  I. Title.
  VA58.4.094   1995
  359'.03'097309045—dc20   94-38465

Printed in the United States of America on acid-free paper ⊚

9 8 7 6 5 4 3

Contents

Preface

This book is about change and innovation in military institutions.

Military organizations, especially successful ones, normally tend to resist change. Order reigns, and there are reasons why this is so. In a very final sense, the lives of the individuals who serve in military organizations depend on other military personnel to act predictably, to be where plans say they should be, at the appointed time, doing what their doctrine and training says they should do. Of course, most organized human activity involves making the actions of its members predictable; what distinguishes military organizations from other institutions, however, is what happens if the rules, plans, doctrine, and behavioral expectations of the organization are not followed. Failure to follow the rules in most nonmilitary organizations can cost time, money, and inconvenience. In military organizations, the costs often are measured in lives and, ultimately, as Jonathan Schell has suggested, the fate of the earth.[1] As a result, military organizations view change and innovation with great caution. The wrong changes, after all, can be fatal, not just for those in uniform but also for their societies.

But sometimes caution can lead to stagnation; and failure to adjust to global changes, advances in military technology, or innovations in the conduct of war can lead to the same kind of disasters that cautious bias about change and innovation was supposed to prevent.

I think we are in such a period. The world swirls with changes that a few years earlier were simply unimagined. The kaleidoscope of international relations seems to twist so much faster now. Technology pushes beyond the frontiers we took as impenetrable limits only a few years ago. The world of incremental change in which we lived in the last four decades has ended, but history has not. In this new era, it is far more dangerous for American military institutions, and for the U.S. Navy in particular, *not* to change.

Acknowledgments

This book reflects discussions, debates, and blue skying with quite a few shipmates over the three decades of my naval career. I am indebted to them all intellectually and conceptually. Listing all those who helped shape the ideas I've expressed in the pages that follow would require a lot more space. There are, however, some people who were of direct help in formulating or critiquing the drafts of the work. I especially want to acknowledge the help, long hours of editing, insights, and visions of Dr. Jim Blaker. Lt. Cdr. Chris Ratliff, Rear Adm. Dave Oliver, Capt. Harry Ulrich, Vice Adm. Hank Mustin, Ambassador Linton Brooks, and Adm. Hunt Hardisty were also of enormous help in clarifying and broadening my understanding of many concepts included in this book. I thank the people at the Naval Institute Press. Fred Rainbow and Mark Gatlin were of immense help, and the skill of the editorial staff, particularly that of Mac Greeley and Anthony Chiffolo, was of the highest professional standards.

My wife, Monika, and my son, Ens. Todd Owens, inspired the best parts of the book, as they have the best parts of my life.

High Seas

Introduction

The dangers we face in the post–Cold War era—regional conflict, weapons proliferation, increased ethnic and nationalistic competition, a decline in the relative economic strength of the nation, and the possible turning away from reform and democracy by Russia or other nations now groping toward democratic governments—may not be the same kinds of direct threats we lived with during the Cold War, but they dictate that military force will continue to be a key instrument for the United States in the years ahead.

To be effective, however, U.S. military forces will have to change. The changes will be defined by how the nation deals with the perennial issues of how much military is enough, what the military structure should look like, what it should do, and how it should do it. But this time the old answers will no longer suffice because the nation has embarked on a quest for a new consensus on national security and the role of military force in preserving it.

Like all the nation's military services, the Navy and Marine Corps have been engaged in this quest since the outline of the new world began to emerge in the late 1980s, marked by the collapse of the Berlin Wall

The former Soviet aircraft carrier Kuznetsov *was the manifestation of what we had prepared for and trained against for decades—Soviet blue-water, sea-control naval power. Now, in the summer of 1991, she had entered the Mediterranean. But she had not come to challenge the Sixth Fleet. She had left the Black Sea because there no longer was a Soviet Union or a Soviet Black Sea Fleet. Her weapons were shrouded and rust crept through her welds. The families of her officers and crew, some with their pets, walked along the deck. As we tracked her through the Mediterranean, I had a poignant feeling of how much the world had changed, and, as she neared the Atlantic, I radioed her captain, Sergei Chekhov, wishing him "fair winds and following seas" for the voyage home. He replied that he no longer knew where home was.*

and the Warsaw Treaty Organization and, ultimately, the breakup of the Soviet Union. The new era, although cloaked in uncertainty, remains one of great promise.

For the Navy, however, the outline was very different intellectually from the one in which our understanding of the world and ourselves was rooted. The changes needed to replace the older understanding have already turned out to be deep, cutting to the core of the operational concept and force planning that had driven thinking inside the Navy for decades.

THE PAST AS PROLOGUE

While the Navy's Cold War world view was publicly announced as "The Maritime Strategy" in 1986, the operational concept it described had actually served as the formal basis for naval planning, doctrine, training, and operations since the end of the Vietnam conflict in the early 1970s. The core of this concept updated Mahan, assumed the U.S. military problem was global, and postulated that the Navy's global maritime mobility could prevent the Soviets from restricting the location of the conflict. While the Soviets might decide when and where the ground conflict would start, U.S. naval forces could define where the maritime battles would be joined. Operationally, the problem was to move the fleet into areas close enough to attack Soviet territory and missile submarines, and then destroy the Soviet forces that contested our control of those seas.

The time was the early 1980s. We were briefing the uniformed Navy four-star hierarchy about the Maritime Strategy and its operational imperatives. Many of the admirals didn't like what we were saying; it was too radical, they thought, even though the basic ideas had been there for more than a decade. It was the idea of articulating them that seemed so controversial. But it occurred to me that it was far more dangerous not to articulate the underlying precepts.

This, we argued, would keep the Soviet Navy away from the U.S. reinforcements flowing across the Atlantic, divert air defense and other Soviet forces away from the fight in central Europe, and, by destroying the Soviet nuclear-powered ballistic-missile submarines, shift the strategic nuclear relationship between the United States and the Soviet Union in favor of the United States.

The Maritime Strategy dominated our thinking long enough for two generations of naval officers to optimize the Navy's weapons and other systems for open-ocean warfare and to create a single Navy view of the world and of itself. Many of the weapons, systems, doctrines, and exercises that define today's U.S. naval forces were forged in the two decades between the U.S. withdrawal from the Vietnam conflict and Operation Desert Storm.

THE SHOCK OF DESERT STORM

Desert Storm, the first post–Cold War conflict, was a magnificent battle—and a doctrinal disaster for the U.S. Navy. Our naval forces performed well. There was no failure of nerve on the part of the men and women who fought there. Desert Storm was a triumph of American military power, and all the military services contributed to that triumph. The Navy was successful, however, largely because it was able to modify its operational doctrine, a doctrine that—along with the weapons, systems, and training it had generated—proved ill-suited to the Gulf War.

Unlike our Army, Air Force, and Marine Corps comrades in arms, we left the first of the post–Cold War conflicts without the sense that our doctrine had been vindicated. Quite the contrary. We left knowing not only that the world had changed dramatically, but that our doctrine had failed to keep pace.

Little in Desert Storm supported the Maritime Strategy's assumptions and implications. No opposing naval forces challenged us. No waves of enemy aircraft ever attacked the carriers. No submarines threatened the flow of men and materiel across the oceans. The fleet was never forced to fight the open-ocean battles the Navy had been preparing for during the preceding twenty years. Instead, the deadly skirmishing of littoral warfare dominated.

Mines relatively close to shore, not submarines in the open ocean, were the primary threat. We did not operate independently hundreds of miles from the Army and Air Force but instead fought with them in the same arena. The weapons, systems, and techniques that we had honed for open-ocean engagements—long-range Phoenix air-to-air missiles, fire-and-forget Harpoon antiship missiles, level-of-effort ordnance planning, decentralized command and control—were all ruled out either by the context of the battle or by the complexities of the sea-land interface in the confined littoral area. For the Navy, more than any other service, Desert Storm was the midwife of change.

THE TRANSITION BEGINS

Change began with difficult questions posed by fleet operators and the Navy staff in Washington: What did strategic deterrence mean in a world in which there was no countervailing military superpower? What did sea control mean when the United States had uncontested control of the seas? What was the real role of naval forces in joint military operations?

The answers boiled down to the most profound challenge to the mainstream of U.S. naval thought since the emphasis on sea control had begun in the early 1970s. By the spring of 1992 a new consensus inside the Navy was forming around these elements: The focus of naval operations should be the littoral, not the open ocean. Naval forces would almost always operate jointly with the Army and the Air Force. We would maneuver *from* the sea, not *on* the sea. Since there was no longer a bona fide challenger to U.S. sea control, power projection would henceforth be the primary focus of naval operations. The Navy and Marine Corps had to be integrated in fact, rather than merely rhetorically. By the fall, these concepts had been formally and publicly stated in a new Navy white paper, ". . . From the Sea," the Navy staff in Washington had been reorganized, and a new programming process, designed to convert the new operational concepts into the reality of forces, was beginning.

Between 1990 and 1993 as much intellectual fermentation and debate took place within the Navy as had occurred at any other time in the twentieth century. As the consensus formed, it was clear that the Navy had to change the way it allocated its resources and trained its forces if the new concepts were to move from rhetoric to reality. Through the summer of 1992 a new Navy staff structure was constructed, and by early 1993 a new decision process for making those allocations was in place. By the spring of 1993 a new target force structure, called Force 2001, began to emerge. This force, the first tangible result of the organizational innovation and intellectual turmoil that began earlier, linked the new operational concept to the size and shape of naval forces. In roughly three years we had set a new course for the nation's naval forces. The way ahead had become clearer, the new assumptions underlying our forces and operations had been accepted, and we began to build the future Navy.

Not everything has been settled, and our thoughts, operational concepts, and force-structure targets will continue to evolve in the years ahead. This is hardly surprising in light of the uncertainties of the future. Nevertheless, we can be more explicit about our vision and goals and about what it will take to reach them. That is the purpose of this book. The following pages try to capture the transition that has occurred inside the Navy since the Berlin Wall was torn down. They yield neither final nor complete answers to the new questions of the era beyond the Cold War, but they do furnish a framework on which the nation can develop more comprehensive answers to the challenges it will face in the future—and the Navy's place in that future.

SOME UNDERLYING ASSUMPTIONS

The views, of course, stem from a particular perspective. My own experience colors them. I'm a submariner, and I've been a fleet commander. I've seen the military from a policy and programming point of view, too, while serving on staffs in the Department of the Navy and the Office of the Secretary of Defense. As the first Deputy Chief of Naval Operations for Resources, Warfare Requirements and Assessment, I was responsible for preparing the Navy Program and budget.

This background helped form the perspective of this book and its underlying assumptions. Since this book is an attempt to be explicit and clear about such things, it is worth stating those assumptions:

—The first is really a hypothesis—that military power is and will remain an important key to the nation's ability to cope with the dangers facing it. This does not mean that military solutions are the only or the best ones, but rather that an international perception of the United States as a potent military power will assist the nation in constructing the best ones.

—The perception of U.S. military power must stem from fact, not rhetoric. Bluff has not been and never should be at the center of U.S. foreign policy; accordingly, the United States must have the military capacity to bring decisive, joint military force to bear against opponents when military action is called for.

—In the years ahead, our military edge will not be manifest in numbers. The size of U.S. forces is going down, and the nation simply does not need the numbers of military personnel, ships, and aircraft or the military infrastructure it built during the Cold War. Instead, our edge will rest increasingly on technical superiority, particularly in high military leverage areas like information warfare, C3I (command, control, communications, and intelligence), surveillance and target acquisition, and standoff precision-guided munitions.

—Military technology in general is advancing at unanticipated rates. U.S. military technology currently leads that of other nations, and the United States will maintain its lead into the future, especially in the capacity to weave these capabilities into effective, meaningful military capability.

—Since there will be no significant challenge to the U.S. Navy's control of the seas for the foreseeable future, U.S. naval forces will focus primarily on influencing events ashore. They must become more flexible and better capable of joint military operations in littoral areas of the world. This will result in a requirement to provide increased direct battlefield support.

—Naval forces will operate differently in peacetime because the underlying rationale for U.S. overseas military presence has changed. The fundamental purpose of U.S. military presence overseas will still be to increase U.S. influence on world affairs, but the foundation for overseas presence will shift away from the extending of a nuclear deterrent umbrella toward different ways of maintaining alliances and enhancing U.S. leadership of bilateral and multilateral coalitions.

—Finally, naval forces increasingly will assume the overall forward-presence role for U.S. forces, and they must alter the way they perform that role, becoming representative not just of U.S. naval power but of the entire range of U.S. military capabilities. In effect, overseas naval forces will become the bridge for U.S. Army and Air Force units to maintain working relationships with their foreign counterparts.

The chapters that follow fall into three broad categories. The first section (chapters 1 through 4) deals with some salient aspects of the new international environment and with what the nation may want to do with its naval forces in this environment. It discusses deterrence, overseas presence, advances in military technology, and ways to coordinate security policy more effectively.

The second section, made up of the single, fairly long chapter 5, draws out the operational implications of the new international context for naval forces. It discusses the ways in which U.S. naval forces will operate with the Army and Air Force in joint military operations, what Navy–Marine Corps integration means, how naval operational configurations will change, and what these considerations imply for undersea, surface, and air operations.

The concluding section (chapters 6 through 9) deals with the size and structure of the naval forces needed to meet the operational imperatives of the new era. It discusses the organizational modifications and the assessment process that helped formulate the Navy's vision of its future forces and describes Force 2001 and what might be called Force 2021. Force 2001 is the target force the Navy will move toward over the remainder of this century; Force 2021 represents the kind of naval forces that could emerge if the United States follows the logic, rationale, and conceptual development begun by Force 2001.

While the United States will face foreign challenges in the years ahead, and we will need effective force to cope with them, I believe, in broad terms, that we face a respite from the kind of military threat to the nation's survival we lived with in the Cold War. That respite could last for years.

Suppose this prognostication were accurate. What general approach should the Navy adopt? We could try to maintain as much of the existing structure, organization, and operational patterns as possible in the face of budget costs and other pressures. What exists now is still quite similar to the force that carried us through the Cold War, and because we designed it

I had gathered all our antisubmarine-warfare experts together to see if it was really true—we simply could not find any Soviet submarines in the Mediterranean. If it was true, it was remarkable; for decades we had tracked, worried about, and planned to cope with the Soviet boats that regularly operated there. It had become a way of life for the Sixth Fleet, and generations of our officers and sailors had dealt with it. Now, all the intelligence we could gather said that the era had ended. There were no Soviet submarines in the Mediterranean. I realized that the Cold War was over.

to deter and counter an opposing military superpower, concerted efforts to keep it might pay off if we had to face such a threat again.

But I believe we should adopt another general approach. We should see this respite as an opportunity, and we should work hard to push the imaginative innovations—in technology, force structure, and doctrine—that can allow us, within about a decade, to move into a new range of military capabilities and build a Navy that will help the United States extend the current respite well into the future.

The argument that lies ahead is straightforward: the nation's naval forces are undergoing an internal revolution of concept and force structure. U.S. naval forces have faced similar periods before and, along with the nation, have worked out new understandings and capabilities to cope with the changes. But the voyage into the next century lies through uncharted, high seas, and the Navy that emerges from this journey early in the twenty-first century will be very different from the one at sea today.

Chapter 1

Deterrence in a Single-Superpower World

The problem was to make sure that Qaddafi's verbal support of Saddam Hussein did not lead to Libyan attacks against the flow of men and materiel through the Mediterranean on the way to Desert Storm. We tried to put ourselves in the Libyan's shoes. It was not easy. What could he do? It seemed to us that taking on the United States would not be rational and could amount to suicide. But would Qaddafi realize how futile it would be? What really deterred someone like him?

Deterrence once anchored debate about how to use U.S. military forces. The term grew from a large compendium of assumptions about a particular international system, a forty-year body of calculations that spelled out the capacities of the United States and Soviet Union to destroy each other. As such, it was a guide to building and using military forces. It helped to determine how many nuclear weapons we needed and how to structure our nuclear capability. It was the logical basis for the strategic nuclear triad. Deterrence also conditioned how we thought about non-nuclear military operations—particularly those that might involve the Soviet Union—using elegant theories of conflict escalation control and dominance.

We no longer talk about deterrence as we once did. The collapse of the world's other military superpower shattered the old connotations of deterrence, and without the bipolar world and the superpower confrontation that fueled international relations, much of the esoteric intellectual superstructure that once went along with deterrence has become archaic. Stripped of its carefully calculated nuclear-destruction probabilities, first-strike scenarios, and the nuances of what we called the nuclear

9

umbrella, the term now rings hollow. Cold War deterrence is no longer a useful guide to building forces or conducting military operations.

In the old bipolar world of mutual assured destruction, each thought the other might seek to opt out of the mutual-suicide pact by trying to destroy the other's retaliatory capability, particularly in periods of rising tension. The old understanding of deterrence connoted a preconflict face-off between hostile nuclear superpowers in which the paramount goal was to avoid direct conflict. Deterrence had failed, we argued, if the United States and Soviet Union ever went to war with each other. If war did break out, escalation control and escalation dominance—concepts that involved fighting a war with another nuclear superpower—were to replace deterrence as operational guides.

Now, however, the United States is the only military superpower. Put bluntly, the United States has the military capacity—in both nuclear and non-nuclear forms—to reverse virtually any military aggression by another nation and to destroy virtually any other nation without risking its own destruction. A single-superpower world makes the older understanding of deterrence useless as a guide for designing and using U.S. military forces.

Yet the United States still threatens to use military force—as opposed to actually employing it—to prevent others from doing things, mostly military things, we do not want them to do. Despite our solo superpower status, we prefer to avoid military conflict and to use our military forces in ways that reduce the chances that we will have to use them for war. Generically, therefore, deterrence still figures in our foreign policy and affects the way we use military force in peacetime. While the context of deterrence is now profoundly different, and the term no longer connotes what it once did, it would be useful to agree on what deterrence means in the new, post–Cold War era. If we had such a common understanding, we could use it as we did the Cold War meaning of deterrence—as a guide for building and using U.S. military forces.

A WORKING DEFINITION FOR THE NEW ERA

With that goal in mind, let me propose a working definition:

> Deterrence refers to how the United States can use its military forces—nuclear and non-nuclear—to dissuade potential opponents from developing or using their military forces in ways the United States finds objectionable.

This definition does several things. It frees the notion of deterrence from the myopia of nuclear use, without, of course, ignoring nuclear weapons. But it is not open-ended. It concentrates on how other nations may try to build and use military forces (including paramilitary forces and state-sponsored terrorist organizations) and does not deal with how an opponent might seek to use nonmilitary organizations or institutions. This does not restrict the United States from attempting to deter a potential opponent from using its diplomats, or its teachers, or its salespeople from taking actions we would object to. It simply says that is a problem for institutions other than the U.S. military to handle.

On the U.S. side, the definition focuses on how to use U.S. military forces to affect the military decisions of potential opponents. The United States should use all the instruments of state authority—diplomacy, propaganda, economic assistance, and trade policies—to deter dangerous military actions by another nation. What I propose, however, is a concept of deterrence that is of particular help in deciding how to size, structure, and operate U.S. military forces to deter a potential opponent from building and using its military forces in ways we would prefer it avoid.

The definition also suggests that deterrence can apply to situations ranging from precrisis to conflict. Because it concerns itself with force-planning decisions by potential opponents, it can deal with events years prior to any military confrontation. We would prefer, for example, that other nations not develop or procure nuclear weapons, and that those that have already done so reduce or abolish the weapons they have. My working definition provides for such an issue by posing questions: what kind of U.S. forces should we build and how should we operate the ones we have to best inhibit nuclear proliferation? Deterrence need not end when war begins. Its primary focus may change depending on when we try to deter actions—perhaps along the lines summarized by table 1:1— but there is no compelling reason why we should stop trying to deter an opponent's actions once we start trying to remove its capability to do them.

TABLE 1:1 Temporal Foci of Deterrence vis-à-vis Potential Opponents

Period	Deterrent Focus
Precrisis	Deter buildup of power-projection forces, acquisition of weapons of mass destruction, and their theater and global delivery systems
Crisis	Deter offensive use of military forces
Conflict	Deter horizontal and vertical escalation; deter other nations from supporting opponent

HOW DETERRENCE WORKS IN THE NEW ERA

The biggest difference from the world we have left behind is the single-superpower status of the United States. This does not mean that the United States is unfettered in its use of military power or more inclined to seek military solutions to international problems. Neither does it mean the elimination of political or moral strictures in the conduct of military operations—nor does it mean that unilateral threats to use its military supremacy would help the United States secure the peaceful, democratic, and prosperous world we would like to see. It does mean that the United States can use the threat of military force differently and perhaps more effectively than it has in the past—if it chooses to do so.

One new aspect of deterrence is that any potential opponent of the United States must assume that it cannot win a military confrontation with the United States, provided the United States has the will to use its military superiority. One could argue that this has been true for some time—and yet it did not deter nations from taking actions opposed by the United States. North Korea and China in the early 1950s, Vietnam in the 1960s, Iran in the 1970s, and Libya in the 1980s all did so.

Each of these, however, occurred in the old bipolar world with all its implications for the spread of conflict and escalation of violence. Whether the United States would use its military superiority decisively was not a question. The North Koreans may have believed the United States had written off Korea as outside the American defensive perimeter. The Chinese may have thought the United States would withdraw from the Korean War when faced with the prospect of large numbers of casualties. Fifteen years later, the U.S. strategy of gradual escalation may have convinced the North Vietnamese that the United States would constrain its use of power to avoid bringing China or the Soviet Union into the conflict more directly.

Yet in each of these cases, what may have been in question was not U.S. power, but—given the nuclear standoff at the time—the will to use it fully. Now the United States often will be able to take decisive action without dwelling excessively on the possible reactions of another superpower to a U.S. use of force. Recent experience and doctrinal statements suggest that the United States will use whatever force is necessary to win a conflict—if it decides to exercise a military option.

That "if" is the key to contemporary military dynamics and to the practical side of deterrence because, in the post–Cold War era, the only reasonable course for an opponent to take in the face of U.S. opposition is to try to erode American willingness to employ its military force.[1] In the near future a potential opponent might seek to

—Take action in such a way as to dramatically change the stakes of a U.S. intervention before the United States intervenes;
—Threaten to cause so many casualties that America would not think the game was worth the candle;
—Threaten a protracted conflict;
—Split any multilateral coalition the United States hoped to incorporate in its response.

The first approach would be a fait accompli strategy. The second raises the specter of weapons of mass destruction. The third attempts to raise the specter of another Vietnam quagmire. The last involves efforts to turn the U.S. desire to work with a supporting coalition into something that inhibits the use of U.S. military power. A smart aggressor would, of course, attempt to use all four strategies to erode the United States's willingness to use its military superiority.

Fait Accompli Aggression

Fait accompli scenarios include situations in which an opponent, realizing that it cannot win a military confrontation with the United States, takes steps to reduce the chances that the United States will intervene militarily by attempting to change the stakes of U.S. military intervention. Consider how Saddam Hussein might have attempted to reincorporate Kuwait as a province of Iraq. Suppose he had moved beyond Kuwait and seized major Saudi Arabian oil facilities before the United States had been able to bring its overwhelming military power to bear. Had he seized control of most of the oil-production capability in the Persian Gulf, he could have presented the United States with a fait accompli that could have changed the stakes of any American effort to force him to retreat. He might believe, for example, that with most of the production capabilities of Saudi Arabia in hand, he could say to the United States, "You can destroy my army and, perhaps, kill me. But before you do that, I can destroy the oil-production facilities on which your standard of living depends. Stay out, and I will guarantee your continued access to Persian Gulf oil, at a lower price than you're paying now. Intervene, and I will deny the Saudi oil resources for fifty years by contaminating them with the nuclear devices I have placed in the Saudi fields; if you intervene, you will lose the oil."

It is not difficult to conjure up any number of such fait accompli scenarios, from North Korea to Bosnia. American planners are not, of course, the only ones who can easily conjure up such dilemmas.

Threatening High U.S. Casualties

Threatening to cause unacceptable casualties if the United States intervenes militarily is also a way of changing the stakes. Making such threats, and trying to make them credible, could become more attractive in the future because we were so successful in limiting friendly casualties in the Gulf War. Our success there might cause potential opponents to assume that any conflict that promises to kill more Americans than were lost in Desert Storm would be particularly hard for the United States to contemplate. But regardless of whether Desert Storm established a casualty ceiling, potential opponents would be right about the American commitment to keep friendly losses as close to zero as possible. The question we now face is whether opponents believe they could exploit the American desire to limit casualties enough to prevent the United States from intervening.

Modern conventional weapons would help regional predators back up this kind of strategy. If they cannot build modern tanks, aircraft, missiles, and the surveillance, radars, and data-processing systems that give them such military potency, regional predators may try to buy their arsenals: all of this deadly military equipment is available on the world market.

Weapons of mass destruction could become particularly attractive. Threats to use chemical, biological, or nuclear weapons were of concern during the Gulf War, and although Iraq never resorted to such weapons, the mere threat complicated U.S. military planning and operations. Postwar evaluating of the Iraqi nuclear-weapons-development program and theorizing on how nuclear weapons might have changed the outcome of Desert Storm heightened the notion that "the next conflict with the United States would involve weapons of mass destruction."[2]

The potential for nuclear proliferation will continue to fuel both general concern for the spread of weapons of mass destruction and specific worries about whether such weapons might neutralize American military superiority. Secretary of Defense Les Aspin told the Senate Budget Committee in February 1993 that nuclear proliferation was the primary danger in the new world-security environment.[3] Since then, the strategic effects of nuclear proliferation have become a major focus within the Pentagon, particularly with regard to the North Korean nuclear program, a key U.S. foreign-policy issue.

Certainly, modern conventional-weapons arsenals and weapons of mass destruction change the risks and therefore the stakes in U.S. military operations. Threats to use them will affect U.S. decisions about intervention in future crises. The question is, can weapons of mass destruction and modern conventional weaponry change the stakes of U.S. military intervention so dramatically in the eyes of potential opponents that they will view U.S. threats to use military force as bluffs?

Rational or not, the United States must be able to deal with threats to use weapons of mass destruction against our military personnel, against friends and allies, or even against the United States itself. Such threats might not deter the United States from intervening, and they could trigger preemptive military action by the United States. The issue is whether the predators believe their threats to use weapons of mass destruction will keep the United States out. If they believe so, our ability to deter them may fail.

Threatening a Protracted Quagmire

America's experience in Vietnam would fascinate any potential aggressors searching for a strategy to prevent the United States from intervening. They might conclude that the prospect of a prolonged conflict would keep the United States out. How might they structure the threat?

They would, of course, say they were willing to engage the United States in a protracted war and proclaim their capacity to do so, referring either to the importance of the goals of their aggression or the commitment of their nations as evidence. But they would have to back up their threats with some evidence that they could, in fact, conduct a protracted war. They might, as Mao Tse-tung did, point to the size of their nations' populations as evidence that they were capable of bearing whatever military wrath the United States might inflict, or point to protracted conflicts in which they had engaged before, as Ho Chi Minh did. Or they might try to structure their forces in such a way to blend with the human and physical terrain where they expected to conduct such a conflict, in effect demonstrating the capacity to conduct guerrilla warfare. They might claim some religious direction—or they might do all of these.

The United States will not ignore such threats. There is ample evidence that Americans do not want to get involved in the open-ended, long-lasting tragedy they overwhelmingly associate with U.S. involvement in Indochina. Regardless of whether aggressors could back up threats to wage protracted war against the United States, they might believe that U.S. sensitivity to the threats would keep the United States from intervening. Like the threats to cause high casualties, what counts is not whether the United States really believes such threats credible. It is whether the aggressors making the threats think they will keep the United States out.

Splitting the Coalition

The United States values coalitions. Desert Storm demonstrated the utility of coping with regional predators within a coalition, and while the United States will be the only military superpower for some time, working with other nations to manage crises has clear benefits. Indeed, there is a logic to coalition operations that goes beyond their most obvious advantages—adding the support of world opinion to the exercise of military power, facilitating access to bases, and spreading the financial burden of military operations. The strategic utility of coalition support for U.S. military operations stems in part from the reality that superpower status generates suspicion and concerns even on the part of friendly nations. No nation is fully comfortable with a single military superpower hanging about because, regardless of the length of their alliance or the compatibility of their interests with those of that superpower, its existence implies to non-superpower nations that their national destiny is not fully theirs to define. The U.S. interest in coalition building, therefore, also flows from our desire to balance the power we have with assurances that we will exercise that power responsibly.

Potential opponents, however, can view the value the United States attaches to maintaining and building international coalitions to deal with crises as an exploitable way of deterring the United States from using its power. Any smart aggressor, for example, would try to divide coalitions that the United States seeks to build, not only to make it more difficult for the United States to bring its military forces to bear, but also in the hope of converting the value the United States ascribes to coalition building into an additional inhibition on deciding to use military force. As a superpower, the United States will be able to do many things unilaterally. But we will prefer to do them in consort with other nations, and any success an opponent has in preventing other nations from joining us will add to our concern about intervening militarily.

MAINTAINING DETERRENCE

These four approaches—the fait accompli, the threat to kill many Americans (or American friends and allies) if the United States intervenes, the threat of a protracted conflict, and efforts to retard or deny coalition support for the United States—are all strategies predators might follow to deter the United States from bringing its military power to bear. If the United States is to deter regional predators, it must find a way to cause them to question whether their efforts to deter U.S. military intervention can possibly succeed.

Countering Fait Accompli Strategies

The most direct way to undermine the credibility of a fait accompli strategy is to increase the risk that it will fail. If predators believe the U.S. can intervene before they are able to present the United States with the intended fait accompli, then they would not be likely to try, for once the United States intervenes, the goal of the strategy—to keep the United States out—has been lost. The key to countering a fait accompli strategy is to build a belief that the United States can and will intervene rapidly.

The need for a quick-response capability is not new. But it is worth noting why it has become more important. In the past, fear of irreversible military loss or the demand to quickly squelch crises that could ultimately involve the two superpowers drove the U.S. desire for this capability. The belief that if the Soviet Union ever successfully occupied Western Europe or the Persian Gulf there was no assurance the United States could evict its forces, drove our concern about the rapid reinforcement of forward-deployed forces in Europe and our interest in building a Rapid Deployment Joint Task Force for Southwest Asia, for example. And for other potential crises, we wanted to be able to respond quickly to resolve the issue before the Soviet Union got involved.

In the new single-superpower era, however, irreversible losses are less plausible because as the only military superpower, the United States can reverse virtually any military gain by virtually any other nation. We can destroy any regional predator, but none of our present potential opponents can do the same to the United States. Do these new-era assumptions make arguments in favor of rapid-response capabilities harder to sustain? If the United States can eventually evict any regional predator from the spoils of aggression, why should we also want to be able to intervene rapidly with military forces?

The answer is that regardless of U.S. military superiority, we would prefer to deter other nations from taking actions we oppose, rather than being forced to engage in open conflict. Even with military superiority, the cost and effort will always be higher to reverse than to deter. The consequences of not being able to respond quickly to crises are not so high as they once were, but the requirement to be able to do so remains compelling.

The deterrent payoff from a rapid-response capability may be even higher now than it was during the Cold War. In the past, few were certain who would win—or whether there would be a winner—if the United States and Soviet Union came to blows. We sought to build a rapid-response capability to be able to deal with crises quickly, before the Soviet Union could intervene and bring about the superpower confrontation we all feared. Even if the United States could respond quickly, however, the outcome was still uncertain: getting there first did not guarantee that we could avoid a clash with another military superpower.

U.S. intervention no longer sets up a potential clash between military superpowers. It sets up a clash between a superior military power and an inferior one, and a U.S. rapid-response capability no longer posits just greater uncertainty about the military outcome. It posits merely an earlier U.S. military victory. This, I think, gives the capacity to respond quickly more deterrent value today than it had before.

How much deterrent value a rapid-response capability generates in the new era, however, depends on several factors. Potential predators must realize that U.S. forces can respond quickly with forces that can defeat a fait accompli strategy. Unfortunately, the scenarios the United States has to worry about revolve around reaction times measured in hours and days rather than weeks or months. The shorter the time the United States has to respond to a fait accompli attempt, the harder it is for the United States to intervene with the level of non-nuclear force clearly able to stop aggressors before they succeed. This generality suggests that a rapid-response force must be powerful enough to make aggressors believe it capable of either stopping or delaying their operational concepts.

U.S. rapid-response forces would probably have to deal with an opponent's ground forces—upon which an aggressor is most likely to rely for a fait accompli attempt. Fait accompli strategies do not have to revolve exclusively around the use of ground forces by the aggressor. Indeed, it is hard to come up with a scenario that would involve only ground forces. It is harder, however, to come up with any scenario that does not depend on the aggressor's ground forces, not only because the nations we worry about trying such a strategy have committed most of their military resources to building and maintaining armies, but also because the strategy itself revolves around gaining control of real estate and holding it at risk. Armies are not the only military force that can hold an asset, a population, or an activity at risk. But the best way to threaten people or things is to hold them, and ground forces are particularly good at doing this. So to undermine fait accompli strategies, we would want to make aggressors believe the United States could intervene with a force sufficient to defeat their ground units, or at least prevent them from carrying out their operational scheme.

There are many ways the United States can affect the ground-force operations of an opponent, and this is not the place to revisit the debates over the efficacy of strategic-bombing campaigns, information warfare, or the myriad of other means the United States could bring to bear against an aggressor's ground forces. The point is more general. If the United States is going to be able to undermine fait accompli strategies, it should focus on how to bring significant force to bear against opponents' ground-force operations rapidly, reduce the impact of any supporting missile or air attacks, and cause opponents to doubt their ability to control their forces. It will be especially important to make potential opponents understand the United States can do these things. This should give us some insights, possibly even vision, about how to build and operate U.S. forces for deterrent purposes.

Trip Wires and Changing the Stakes of a Fait Accompli Attempt

Opposing ground forces with ground forces is a direct approach. Ground units are not the only military force that can deal with opposing ground forces, but opponents' calculations about their ground operations are bound to be affected strongly by how quickly they believe the United States can intervene with our ground forces. U.S. ground-force intervention carries another connotation, too, for it is the stuff of trip wires and the most obvious way the United States can implement the other generic way of undermining fait accompli strategies: namely, changing the stakes of a confrontation before the opponent can. Ground forces can do this because, of all our forces, they express the solidity of the U.S. commitment: once committed, they are the most difficult to withdraw, and once committed in the face of an aggressor's army, they are the most likely to suffer casualties. The aggressor is likely to believe that a clash with U.S. ground forces, and the U.S. casualties that may stem from such a clash, could well change the U.S. stakes from protecting U.S. interests to avenging American lives.

Unfortunately, this approach raises the prospect of human trip wires. Stationing massive ground forces more or less permanently in every potential hot spot is not really an option, and whereas we obviously must invest heavily in strategic mobility, no amount of air and sea lift or prepositioning can by itself erase the interest of potential opponents in surprise attacks. The faster the need for U.S. ground forces to be put in place, the fewer forces can be there when needed. And the fewer forces there when the confrontation begins, the more likely those forces will be unable to prevail, and the more likely they will function as trip wires. This has always been hard to sell in American military planning.

How does the United States enhance its ability to deploy ground forces quickly without relying on a trip-wire strategy? The key is to develop the capacity to support the ground forces with enough firepower, mobility, intelligence, and logistics to give them a fighting chance against the numerically superior forces they may confront. The deterrence goal in the face of a fait accompli attempt is, after all, to build a belief in the mind of predators that the United States can disrupt or delay their operational schemes enough to prevent them from changing the stakes of the confrontation before the U.S. has intervened in a big way militarily. We can do this by raising the prospects of rapid U.S. ground-force intervention. But we can disrupt and delay predators' ground-force operational schemes by attacking their supporting forces and their command and control systems as well.

In the end, to deter a regional predator from attempting a fait accompli strategy, the United States needs the visible capacity to respond quickly enough to undermine this strategy. The military response capability with the greatest deterrent value in this context is one that threatens to prevent, disrupt, or delay the aggressor's ground-force operations. The visible ability to intervene rapidly with U.S. ground forces probably has particular effect, but there will be a tough tradeoff between the speed of intervention required and the strength of the ground force introduced. To skirt the thorny issue of human trip wires, the United States should supplement the inherent power of its ground forces with fire support, intelligence, surveillance, mobility, and agility provided by forces not deployed ashore with them.

In the more distant future, it may be possible to undercut a potential adversary's interest in a quick ground-force territorial grab without relying on ground-force trip wires. We should move in that direction, toward a broad range of surveillance, strike, and defensive capabilities that, together with strategic mobility, can raise the risk of ground-force operational failure in the minds of potential predators.

This would involve a four-pronged capability:

—Wide-area defensive systems to neutralize aggressors' air and missile support for their ground forces;
—Enough long-range precision strike weapons to hold critical sensitivities including command and control at risk;
—Battlefield fire-support systems featuring sensor-fused submunitions that can prevent mobile armored forces from carrying out their missions;
—Information warfare capable of degrading predators' awareness and understanding of the course of their ground-force operations.

The visible assembly of these kinds of capabilities would help immeasurably to prevent potential predators from believing they could pull off a ground-force-based fait accompli.

Countering a Threat to Kill Americans

Whether the opponent backs up a threat to inflict high casualties on intervening U.S. forces with modern conventional weapons or weapons of mass destruction, the most direct way of undermining it is to have invulnerable forces. That is a difficult challenge. There are ways we can move in that direction, however, and—important for deterrence—ways we can make predators believe their threats to kill Americans are vacuous. That predators know such threats are hollow will not stop them from bluffing. It will, however, make it harder for them to risk incurring the wrath of the United States.

Some ways of moving toward relatively invulnerable forces have been around since the beginning of warfare. To the extent that one force can gain and expand an edge over another in the capacity to move quickly, strike at greater distances with greater accuracy and precision, strike more often with devastating weapons, and avoid, deny, or delay the opposing force's efforts to do the same, that force becomes relatively invulnerable. At the most basic level, this phenomenon has been an issue of technology and a willingness to innovate. Military technology—the capacity to convert the understandings provided by science to practical military use—provides the means to create these kinds of edges. But a willingness to innovate—the capacity to use the technology in different ways—determines the degree of edge.

The regional predators we may wish to deter probably cannot erode the U.S. technological edge in conventional weaponry. This judgment is controversial. A glance at the newspapers or a tour of the air, naval, and army shows throughout the world gives the impression that virtually any level of military technology is now available to any nation that has the money and interest in buying it. Such an impression is misleading. What appears as a cornucopia of modern weapons and military systems for less-developed nations is really a signal of the edge in the technology of the developed nations. Nations such as Iraq, Iran, and Libya can buy sophisticated aircraft. Yet because they lack the scientific and production base to design, test, and produce such aircraft, they cannot exceed the technology of the aircraft they buy from the nations that produce them. Unless they have the kind of pilot-training and maintenance infrastructure possessed by advanced industrial nations, they will not be able to use the aircraft as effectively. Nations that produce sophisticated aircraft for sale abroad invariably also produce or can produce more sophisticated, more capable aircraft for themselves.

The real technological edge between a nation like the United States and a potential regional predator is that the United States understands the modern weapons better than the purchaser. Was the integrated air defense Iraq bought from the French a threat to the American pilots who flew against it? Clearly, yes. But was that system also a vulnerability to the Iraqis because they relied on it to defend against U.S. aircraft, and because the Americans understood the system—its strengths and weaknesses—well enough to neutralize it? Perhaps. My hypothesis is that higher-level technology that regional predators can buy, but cannot produce indigenously, does not automatically reduce the U.S. military technological edge. Such technology may in fact constitute an exploitable vulnerability.

In any case, there are some areas of military technology in which the United States is likely to remain unapproachable for some time. One is the ability to exploit space-based systems. Another is the ability to collect, collate, analyze, and understand what is militarily significant from vast amounts of raw information, a function in part of computer technology, but one that stems ultimately from the kind of global perspective and systems possessed by the United States—and by no other nation. Another is the ability to rapidly transfer and use vast amounts of information throughout the U.S. military.

These advantages give the United States high military leverage. In today's jargon, they allow the United States to work within an opponent's decision cycle—to know, understand, and exploit an opponent's decision and command processes. In effect, this enables the United States to know more about what its opponents will try to do, and when they will try to do it, than the opponents can know about the United States. And that will allow the United States not only to focus its offensive capabilities on where the opponents are most vulnerable, but to prevent the opponents from knowing the vulnerabilities of the opposing U.S. forces. This is systemic stealth. It permits the United States to make its military forces relatively invulnerable to those of any currently conceivable opponent.

But what about the prospect that regional predators may be armed with nuclear weapons? Sometimes called the great equalizers in military relationships, they certainly add a new dimension to the threat to kill Americans.

Despite the justified concern over proliferation, we should not lose perspective about what it means for nations like Iraq, Iran, North Korea, or others to acquire nuclear weapons, at least over the next decade. These countries will not be able to destroy the United States but will risk retaliatory destruction themselves. The significance of that ground truth is that threats of employing weapons of mass destruction against U.S. forces, or even against the United States itself, ultimately come up against reality: the stakes in a nuclear confrontation with the United States are stacked against our opponents. They may be able to cause apprehension and fear by such threats, but they can entertain no hopes for controlling the inevitable escalation and, therefore, face utter destruction. The United States should certainly work hard to prevent nuclear-weapons proliferation, but it is neither rational nor helpful to portray a few nuclear or chemical weapons in the hands of some regional power as capable of neutralizing American military superiority.

In undermining opponents' claim that they can impose unacceptable casualties on the United States, however, the issue is not which nation can inflict the most damage. The real issue is whether opponents believe they can extract enough casualties to make the United States believe a confrontation is not worth the costs. (A confusion on this distinction was one of the errors of our strategy in the Vietnam War.) The challenge of deterrence is to convert our relative invulnerability into an opponent's belief that our invulnerability is nearly absolute. Doing this will require much work before and during a crisis. Basically, we must demonstrate our technological edge regularly in exercises and other ways that reinforce the image of U.S. invulnerability.

Countering the Threat of a Protracted Military Quagmire

How can the United States make potential opponents believe we discount their threats of a protracted war if we intervene? Part of the answer involves stated U.S. policy. Documents such as the National Security Strategy of the United States say, among other things, that the United States will not allow protracted conflict. And the term "decisive force," often used by U.S. defense officials specifically to connote the U.S. intention to end any conflict in which it engages quickly, signals it also.

More important in undercutting threats of protracted war, however, is for the United States to field forces that can bring decisive power to bear. Adequate, well-trained, fully ready active military forces are key. If poorly trained or equipped forces must fight while the nation mobilizes its reserves, prolonged conflict and excessive American deaths become more likely.

Combat-ready active forces are probably not enough to convince predator that quagmire threats will not work. Our forces also must have certain characteristics—and these turn out to be similar to those required to undermine other kinds of threats: a visible rapid-response capability coupled with relative invulnerability. Thus the same patterns of overseas deployment that provide visible evidence of a quick response to a fait accompli attempt also serve to ensure that predators never get to fight a long war—because they will lose the short war.

Perceived invulnerability also undercuts threats of protracted conflict. Threatening to prolong a conflict is really just another way of threatening to kill many Americans, albeit fewer at a time over a longer period. If the predator views U.S. forces as relatively invulnerable because of their technological edge, the threat of protracted conflict loses its bite. To the extent that a predator understands that even prolonged conflict will not lead to excessive loss of life, it strengthens deterrence.

Countering Efforts to Split U.S.-Led Coalitions

Even if they are uncertain they can split a U.S.-led coalition, aggressors almost certainly will try to limit the extent to which other nations lend support to U.S. military operations. Their efforts may take the form of direct threats to other nations if they provide base access or other forms of support to U.S. military operations. They may also be more ambiguous and involve long-term efforts to erode the status and character of the United States in the eyes of other nations.

The success of these efforts is likely to be a function of the relationship between the United States and other nations before the crisis surfaces. If the United States has a reservoir of trust with potential coalition partners, efforts to erode support for the United States are less likely to be successful. Likewise, if the United States cultivates an understanding of its military capabilities among potential coalition partners before the crisis, a predator's threats against them in that crisis will have less influence on their actions. In other words, the ability of the United States to undermine a potential opponent's efforts to isolate the United States from international support in a crisis depends on how the United States acts before the crisis. It also depends on the extent to which the United States can help protect its coalition partners during the crisis, thereby negating the opponent's threats against them.

The United States has a long history of peacetime operations designed to build trust with allies. The challenge is to take advantage of that experience and adapt it to the demands of the new era. The United States is up to that challenge, but it is no longer a matter of business as usual.

The USS *Mississippi* launches a Tomahawk Land Attack Missile during Desert Storm. The long-range, precision-attack capabilities represented by such systems will be a key to deterrence in the years ahead.

SOME IMPLICATIONS FOR FORCES AND OPERATIONS

Undermining the various counterdeterrence strategies a potential opponent may adopt, then, carries a number of implications both for the kinds of military forces the nation needs and for how we should operate our forces. The arguments laid out above suggest that the best deterrent forces would be perceived as

—Capable of responding quickly to disrupt, delay, or defeat a regional predator's ground-force operational scheme;
—Able to do this without sustaining heavy casualties;
—Able also to help protect possible coalition forces.

Meeting the first criterion would weaken the attraction of the fait accompli strategy. The second would undercut an opponent's threat to make the cost of U.S. military intervention too high and, in conjunction with the first, can vitiate threats to protract a conflict. The third makes it hard for an opponent to turn the U.S. desire to avoid acting unilaterally into an inhibition on any action. Forces that meet these three criteria could not, of course, guarantee deterrence, but forces that meet these criteria are of higher deterrent value than those that do not.

The three criteria also tend to rule out certain kinds of forces from deterrence roles. Reserve forces, for example, probably cannot meet the rapid-response requirement, nor can heavy ground forces not already close enough to be employed quickly. Naval forces that can attack an opponent's ground forces are more useful for deterrent purposes than naval forces that cannot. Vulnerable air power has less deterrent potential than air power we can apply with less risk.

It would be wrong to push this into either-or differentiation and toward conclusions that naval forces or air forces are best for deterrence purposes. Few U.S. operations have seen a single service provide all the forces, and there are likely to be fewer, if any, such operations in the future. Indeed, no single service is even theoretically capable of meeting all three criteria better than the other services in all situations.

A quick response can be a function of position and technology. Naval forces poised off the coast may be able to respond most quickly in some cases; long-range Air Force bombers, stationed in the United States, may be able to respond first in others. The ability to disrupt an opponent's ground operations may be more a function of the national capacity to identify, track, and target those ground forces than what any single force component can bring to bear against them, and the capacity to hold coalitions together in the face of an opponent's efforts to split them may have much more to do with the success of American diplomacy than with American military prowess.

The character and success of deterrence are, of course, related to how we use military force. The core of force use has been and will remain the manipulation of violence. We design our forces to fight; that we see military force as a powerful destructive instrument of policy is what ties them to deterrence. The way we use our military units in exercises, or in what we call normal peacetime activities, is therefore a form of communication. It signals to those we may wish to deter how we can use military power.

Chapter 2

The Use of Military Force and Overseas Presence

The Bulgarian was at least eighty years old. He stood on the pier, his hand resting on the side of the Sixth Fleet flagship, as the captain and I walked toward him. Our interpreter asked what he was doing. He replied that he had waited forty-five years for the Sixth Fleet to bring America to Bulgaria, and he was savoring the moment, both for himself and hundreds of his friends who had died waiting for this day. It was the way he said it, I think, that suddenly filled that old saw about naval forces showing the flag with strong human meaning. To that weathered old man, the concept was far from a cliché.

Since the end of the Korean War, the United States has maintained between one-quarter and one-third of its military establishment forward-deployed in ground, air, and naval units. The number of U.S. military personnel stationed overseas has varied from year to year, but on average—and excluding the military buildup in Vietnam in the 1960s—the United States has deployed about half a million active U.S. military personnel abroad for more than four decades. This level of peacetime overseas presence was unprecedented before midcentury, but after the United States emerged as a world superpower at the end of World War II, it became the norm. We saw the capacity and willingness to maintain a sizable overseas military presence as a mark of our superpower status.

For most of the last fifty years the U.S. military presence overseas was predicated on a particular understanding of military-force use. Now, with the world so different, is that understanding of the use of force the one we should maintain? It is a question worth pondering.

27

THE USE OF MILITARY FORCE IN THE NEW ERA

For nearly thirty years a debate concerning the uses of U.S. forces has smoldered within the military. It began in the Vietnam conflict. The tragic bombing of the Marine Corps barracks in Lebanon rekindled it in the 1980s. It continued after Desert Storm and today underlies discussions about whether the United States should use military forces in places like Bosnia and Somalia.

For the most part, the debate has addressed ambiguous situations rather than contingencies that military planners considered likely or in which U.S. interests were relatively clear. There was, for example, a broad national consensus that the United States should commit its military forces to combat if the Soviet Union attacked the United States or our allies. Our strategic nuclear strategy rested on the assumption that our retaliation against a nuclear attack on the United States would be certain. We debated internally the nature of the retaliation, but there was no doubt that we would commit military forces to combat. Similarly, we debated little about whether the United States should commit its forces to combat if the Warsaw Pact attacked Western Europe, or if North Korean forces attacked the Republic of Korea. The forces we stationed in Europe and Korea were bound to be involved in these situations, making moot the issue of whether we should commit them to combat. Yet there was considerable room left for discussion, rhetoric, emotion, and debate over whether and when the United States should use military force in a large range of other situations.

The mainstream view within the military today is in part a reaction to the Vietnam conflict. Driven largely by widespread disenchantment with that experience, it calls for great caution in committing U.S. military forces to combat, but relatively unconstrained force use if committed. Secretary of Defense Caspar Weinberger probably articulated the perspective best in the early 1980s in what some called the Weinberger Doctrine. Picking up many of the views of the professional military at the time, he argued that the United States should not commit its military forces to combat unless the use of those forces was "vital to U.S. national interests, or to the interests of U.S. allies," and

—the political and military objectives of the commitment were clearly defined,
—the commitment would be supported by the Congress and the American people, and
—the commitment was the last resort.

The Weinberger Doctrine also said that if the United States decided to commit U.S. forces to combat, the commitment "should be made wholeheartedly, and with the clear intention of winning." This was not, of course, an argument in favor of spending lives and treasure without restrictions. Wholehearted pursuit of the war aims did not mean fighting without regard to the number of American lives that might have to be sacrificed. Instead, the assumption was that conflict was necessarily going to involve great danger to the forces the United States committed to combat. This assumption carried the implied admonition to win quickly, for the longer the conflict continued, the more likely it was that U.S. casualties would grow and U.S. public support for the commitment would erode.

The Weinberger Doctrine's association with the notion of overwhelming force, then, stemmed from the desire to end conflict quickly and completely and to assure, as much as possible, that it would not be necessary to commit U.S. forces again over the same issue or against the same opponent. It is not really fair to try to capture the richness of the thought that went into the doctrine with a single statement. But if it could be done, it would go something like this: "Be very cautious about committing U.S. forces to combat, but when you must commit them, do so overwhelmingly."

Toward a Pragmatic Concept of Force Use

The Weinberger Doctrine dominated American military thinking after the Vietnam conflict—for at least two decades, now—and its intellectual roots reach much further back in American history. Yet I think that it may no longer be the only guide and that it is time to consider an alternative. Let's call it the pragmatic view.

The pragmatic "doctrine" of force use starts from the assumption that the changes in the world—particularly the coincidence of Soviet collapse with the military technical revolution in the United States—have changed the utility and undercut some of the assumptions of the Weinberger Doctrine. The pragmatic view, of course, carries a set of its own presumptions, namely, that

—the link between international developments and national security is more ambiguous now;
—the United States can use its military forces effectively, without risking heavy casualties;
—a commitment of U.S. forces to conflict can be revoked with relatively small political cost;
—credible, proportional use of force, when required, is an important element in demonstrating U.S. will to be an effective deterrent and coalition partner and is, therefore, in the long-term national interest.

The end of the bipolar world makes it harder to perceive links between events overseas and U.S. national security. This is not to argue that the connection between international developments and national security was always direct and clear. Nor is it to suggest that international events have little effect on U.S. national security, or that national security should no longer be a prime concern of U.S. foreign policy. But the fact is that when we assumed a global confrontation between the United States and the Soviet Union, it was much easier to define which crises or developments threatened our security. We could talk reasonably about how events would affect the relationship between ourselves and the opposing military superpower. In short, the gauge we had for judging whether to use U.S. military forces was never precise, but it rested on a broad consensus on why the use of force would be necessary. We Americans had a national sense of when we should use military force, and we had a pretty good idea of what the results of force use would be.

Now, what constitutes a threat to the security of the nation and where we should use military force is much more ambiguous. No longer engaged in a global contest with another military superpower, we no longer have a straightforward, reasonable gauge to define what constitutes a threat to our national security—and what does not. With the link between national security and developments overseas much fuzzier, the goals for which we should commit military forces to combat are less clear.

So, what if the link between events abroad and U.S. national security is more ambiguous now? Greater ambiguity does not equate automatically to greater danger.

It may, however, lead to a more chaotic world and, when coupled with the Weinberger Doctrine, could encourage regional predators. If the dynamics of deterrence in today's single-superpower world are as I suggested, for example, then potential predators, believing the United States will agonize for weeks or months over whether it can commit forces to combat, may be more willing to try what I described as a fait accompli strategy. We may already have had one demonstration of this hypothesis.

In a March 1990 speech Saddam Hussein addressed what the end of the bipolar world meant to Iraq. It meant, he argued, that Iraq could no longer depend on the support and backing of a superpower and would have to rely on its own strength in pursuit of its national interests. But, he suggested, if Iraq could no longer depend on support from the Soviet Union, so too was it no longer dependent on the Soviet Union. The end of the bipolar world allowed Iraq to seek its interests unfettered by the constraints of a superpower's prior approval.[1] Later, as the decision to invade Kuwait approached, did Saddam convince himself that the United States would not commit its forces against him because the Iraqi action would not constitute a clear threat to the United States and, as such, U.S.

intervention would not meet the tests set by the Weinberger Doctrine?

The effect of the Weinberger Doctrine in ambiguous situations was challenged almost as soon as Weinberger enunciated his views. Secretary of State George Shultz and others, for example, suggested that meeting all the tests set up by the doctrine before committing U.S. forces would clearly be time consuming, if it could be done at all. If the doctrine prohibited quick responses to aggression, then America might ultimately lose more lives. Moreover, it would undercut U.S. diplomacy if other nations believed the United States would almost never be willing to use its military power. In Shultz's view, "the hard reality is that diplomacy not backed with strength will always be ineffectual at best, and dangerous at worst."[2] Such critiques had a ring of truth in the bipolar world. They are even more persuasive now.

Has the danger of committing U.S. forces to combat lessened, and have the costs of withdrawing forces before they win changed in this new era? The answer, I think, is a qualified yes. Committing forces to combat will never be risk-free, and withdrawing them before they have achieved the goal of the original commitment will always have negative political ramifications. But these are relative issues, and we should recognize that the context of the use of force has changed so much that our earlier assumptions about risks and costs may now be invalid.

In the context of the bipolar confrontation, the use of U.S. military forces abroad usually carried the potential for escalation, ultimately into a society-killing nuclear exchange. To be sure, this potential was often quite limited. But in the context of zero-sum interactions with another nuclear superpower, the specter of conflict escalation was always there. That backdrop also raised the stakes of withdrawing committed forces, for we saw the unsuccessful use of military force as an international loss of great portent, not just as a mistake. Indeed, it was this bipolar background that gave the Weinberger Doctrine such intellectual power, for if the stakes of military use were ultimately tied to the survival of the nation, and if withdrawing those forces without having achieved the goals for which they were committed affected the power relationship with an opposing military superpower, then the doctrine's precepts—great caution in committing forces in the first place, the need to commit overwhelming force, and no withdrawal without success—all made sense.

Two corollaries also made sense in this high-stakes context. First, we associated force use almost exclusively with national security. To be sure, we Americans sometimes used military forces in situations in which the threat to the nation was not necessarily direct, immediate, or clear. But we saw those as exceptions and believed strongly that unless our national security was threatened, the use of military force was less justified. Second, we accepted the use of force as a final resort, something that was most legitimate after other means of suasion—diplomacy, economic pressure, and threat—had first been tried. We thought of committing U.S. forces to conflict as a final step in a sequence of actions.

This sequential view of the use of military force was not simply a reflection of the Cold War background. Alfred Thayer Mahan, the godfather of American naval doctrine, had argued similarly at the end of the nineteenth century. Nor was it a uniquely American view. European military theorists accepted the notion that a resort to arms should occur only after taking other steps. What is more important, Soviet military theorists agreed throughout the 1960s, 1970s, and 1980s with the basic precept. Only the Chinese, in the 1960s, argued that the use of military force was not necessarily a last resort, suggesting that rather than war being an extension of politics, politics actually grew "out of the barrel of a gun."[3] But such philosophical challenges could be, and were, dismissed by most American theorists and, eventually, by the Chinese themselves. So, for decades the United States worked within an international security system in which the major protagonists accepted the same set of rules regarding the use of military force.

But now what? Many of the assumptions of the past remain valid for some kinds of situations. It still makes a great deal of sense to be cautious about force commitments. The consequences of any military-force use will always be serious, for the essence of military force will always revolve around deadly violence. Because of this, it is normally wise to lean in favor of exhausting other means of suasion before resorting to what some call the final arbiter—military force.

For some situations. It makes the most sense for situations that are clearly fraught with peril to the forces we may commit. It made sense when Iraq invaded Kuwait, for although the final military confrontation in Desert Storm produced remarkably few coalition casualties, it was clear that the scale of the military operations, the level of force involved, and the modernity of the weapons we confronted made the commitment of force perilous to those deployed. In short, we should not discard the sequential approach to the use of military force—in high-risk situations.

But what of the more likely, lower-risk situations in the years ahead? Does the logic of using military force as a final resort make as much sense in cases like Libya in the early 1980s? Or Noriega's Panama? I do not think so. In cases like these the normal sequence of interaction, based on the assumption that the use of military force should be a last resort, may work against us. On some occasions a far more effective—and ultimately less costly—approach may be to use military force as a complementary element, along with the economic and diplomatic steps we now tend to think of as precursors to military force. In effect, of course, this would mean a greater U.S. willingness to use military force earlier in some situations than has been the case in the past. In some cases, however, it may be the right thing to do.

This is not a call for using military force early simply because the object of our concern is so relatively weak that we can assert our military power with very little risk to ourselves. It simply recognizes that many of those whose actions we want to influence, curtail, or compel may not operate within the same set of ethical, political, economic, and social assumptions that color our thinking about the use of military force. Aideed in Somalia, the military hierarchy in Haiti, or the factional leaders in Bosnia are products of another set of assumptions, bound in ethnic or historical dilemmas that ignore our entreaties, threats, or economic sanctions. To influence the behavior of such people, we might demonstrate our concerns more readily in ways they may better understand. This could mean using military force earlier and in different ways than we have usually considered.

Do the actions of people like Aideed or the factional leaders in Bosnia threaten the security of the United States, and if they do not, should we consider the use of military force in dealing with them? In the past, we might have seen their actions as constituting national-security threats because of the bipolar context in which we interpreted virtually all international events. Not too long ago we thought a civil war in Yugoslavia—similar to the real one that broke out after the collapse of the Warsaw Treaty Organization—could be the fuse for armed conflict between the East and West. As such, we imbued a civil war in the Balkans with immediate national-security implications.[4] Now, of course, such escalatory security scenarios seem sadly out of place, and situations we may deplore on moral, political, or humanistic grounds are harder to envision as direct threats to the nation's security.

This does not mean the United States should automatically exclude the use of military forces in trying to influence such situations. Military force is essentially an instrument of U.S. policy, and if it is U.S. policy to alter deplorable situations, we should consider the credible, prudent use of all the means we have to implement that policy, including military force. Indeed, while situations that work against our interests and values may not be immediate security threats to the nation, they can eventually create an international environment that will generate more immediate threats. It may be in the nation's strategic, long-term interest to deal with them even if doing so requires us to use military force. It is clearly in the national interest to make this new era safer and better. If using military force can facilitate reaching that goal, then we should not exclude thinking about how to best use military force in altering deplorable situations or in doing the right thing.

Is not the commitment of U.S. military forces, in fact, more revocable? Because we are no longer in a zero-sum game with another superpower, the stakes of withdrawal from combat situations are not so high as we once saw them. Is not the commitment of U.S. forces less risky to those committed? I think so, not only because the commitment is easier to revoke, but also because more and more we have the power and the technological capability to control the character of most conflicts we are likely to encounter for the foreseeable future. As such, the use of American military forces does not have to be so inherently dangerous to those forces as it once was.

Nor so dangerous to those noncombatants who may surround the thugs, predators, or dictators we wish to affect by using force. U.S. military force can be applied with increasing precision in the years ahead in ways that can affect precisely those we wish to affect, without harming others. This is one of the most important policy implications of the military technological revolution, for the combination of high-technology information management, real-time intelligence and surveillance, and long-range, quick-response, precision-guided weapons will allow us to discriminate in the way we apply military power beyond what was recently imaginable, challenging the near-axiom that collateral damage is a necessary component of combat operations. Indeed, we will soon be able to think seriously about the long-range application of non-lethal force and information warfare, concepts that will ultimately change the basic understanding of what the application of military force means altogether.

What are the international implications of military-force use and the revocation of its use in this new era? Single-superpower status can breed resentment simply because other nations do not feel comfortable with the situation. The United States must use its superpower status carefully, and in ways that engender trust. We must convince other nations that we will remain self-regulating. On the other hand, the appearance of weakness or paralysis can be just as strong a stimulant for other nations to challenge us as an overbearing appearance.

These considerations bear directly on the issue of how and when to use U.S. military forces in the new era. One could argue that self-regulation requires us to avoid unilateral military actions, employ military forces only in consort with coalition partners, and invoke the use of force only with the agreement of those partners. How we deal with coalitions will affect how we can deal with them in subsequent crises. But that generality must be dealt with on a case-by-case basis. Keeping them fully informed is crucial: no one likes surprises. Yet we must not allow our decision-making flexibility to be unduly curtailed by coalition concerns. Admittedly, this is a fine line, but we should not lose sight of the basic dynamic of coalition building. Other nations will join us in coalitions because they share the same goals and trust us. They will also join us because we are willing to lead.

The Dual Doctrine for the Use of Military Force

We may soon develop a dual doctrine regarding the use of military force. Many of the ideas embodied in the Weinberger Doctrine will remain as guides for the use of U.S. military force in the kind of high-risk, major regional contingencies that dominate planning and form our basic understanding of the required military capabilities. Along with these guidelines, however, it would not be surprising to see the pragmatic approach emerge as a doctrine applicable to the more likely, less risky contingencies that are not immediate threats to the security of the nation, but in which the use of force—not as a last resort, but in concert with other policy instruments—promises to correct a deplorable humanitarian situation or lead to a better international environment.

We should base our guidelines for using military force in these situations on an appreciation of the strength and character of Americans, who have not shirked from using military force when they believed its use was just. This sense of justice clearly encompassed defending our security from immediate external threats.

The American sense of just-force commitment, however, also extends beyond immediate self-protection and includes the broader concepts of humanitarianism and the promotion of democratic ideals. It looks to the future. Americans are an altruistic people. Doing what seems to be the right thing resonates with us, perhaps more broadly and deeply than with many other nations. We maintain an open society and government—more open than most—because we believe we can distinguish reason from rhetoric, can judge the validity of the cascade of arguments our system promotes, and can discern the best solution to problems.

Our doctrine for the use of military force must reflect this American character, particularly in those situations that do not constitute an immediate security threat to the nation. Such situations may not demand the prior approval of Congress before committing military forces, intermeshed with other economic, political, and diplomatic instruments. But above all, the decision and action should be explained to Congress and the American people in very short order. The following guidelines might apply:

—Concisely and openly define the goal of the action specifically and explain the mission of the forces committed clearly. This explanation must address how the military mission fits with other U.S. economic, political, and diplomatic actions.

—Set explicit criteria for ending the military actions. These criteria should address more than the success of the mission. They also should address what happens if the mission does not accomplish all its objectives.

—Make the general campaign plan explicit. Explain it to the public if possible and to the civilian leadership if not. Design the campaign plan specifically to take full advantage of our high-technology capabilities in surveillance, mobility, and precision weapons and reduce the risk to U.S. personnel.

—Explain explicitly how the action fits into U.S. immediate and longer-term interests.

THE USE OF FORCE AND OVERSEAS PRESENCE

How the United States thinks about the use of military force will affect the kind of forces it builds and the disposition of those forces abroad. This has been the case in the past; it will continue to help shape the character, location, and purposes of U.S. overseas military presence. It will not be the only thing that affects overseas presence. History, tradition, alliances, and the configuration of international politics also will play important roles.

We often associate overseas military presence with crisis response, in part because military planners often assume overseas presence allows more rapid response to crises. Military presence is, however, less specific than crisis response. It involves a less episodic use of military force and a regularity of activity. It is the technical term for showing the flag and an important means of demonstrating continuing interest, providing deterrence, building coalitions, developing knowledge of the playing field, or indicating foreign-policy concerns.

Although it has many uses, the purpose of overseas presence should not be ambiguous, and we should use appropriate forces to maintain it. We should be clear about why we want to maintain an overseas military presence and about the kinds of forces that can best serve those purposes.

The Changing Context of U.S. Overseas Presence

The driving rationale for U.S. overseas military presence over most of the last half century was the policy of containment. Not all U.S. overseas deployments during the Cold War were a direct expression of that policy, but the basic character and location of U.S. overseas presence clearly reflected it. We commonly used the phrase "forward deployments" because it captured the notion of forces stationed on a distant frontier, along the border of an opponent seeking aggrandizement. Specifically, U.S. overseas presence tended to flow from and respond to the disposition of Soviet military forces. Because the Soviet Union deployed large ground forces in Eastern Europe, structured to attack into the West, the United States maintained the bulk of its forward-deployed Army forces in Western Europe. Because the character and location of Soviet forces changed incrementally and slowly, at least until the 1990s, there was a stability to U.S. peacetime overseas presence as well.

Four decades ago, Army personnel made up about two-thirds of all the U.S. military personnel deployed overseas. This holds roughly true today. Four decades ago, the U.S. Navy began to operate forward from three hubs: general deployment areas in the Atlantic, Pacific, and Mediterranean that remained the same year after year. Today, those deployment hubs still characterize most U.S. naval overseas deployments (with the addition of the Indian Ocean–Arabian Sea as a hub in the 1980s). U.S. overseas basing also has been remarkably stable.

It is true that the number of overseas bases used by the United States has decreased incrementally and steadily since the U.S. withdrawal from Vietnam. Considered globally, this decline is best understood as a contraction to the basing centers in Europe, Japan, and Korea established following World War II. The bases in use today are located almost without exception in the same countries where the United States had bases forty years ago, when the policy of containment emerged.

The collapse of the Soviet Union ended containment as a driving rationale. Overseas military deployments are no longer necessary to contain Russia, which will be occupied for some time with avoiding further fragmentation, not territorial expansion, and the United States does not need overseas bases to prevent the rise of another antagonistic nuclear superpower. Overseas presence now is needed fundamentally to help consummate the transition to what the end of the bipolar international system makes possible: a world in which the United States and other nations can pursue their interests in mutually beneficial ways, less conditioned by fear of conflict, less constrained by disagreements on the rules of international interaction.

This transition is not assured. Ethnic

It was the first visit of the Sixth Fleet flagship to Sevastopol. A hard-line communist had come on board, and I was listening as one of the ship's junior officers explained the capabilities of an air-defense missile system. "Yes, yes," said the Russian official, "I know all about the American offensive systems. That's all you Americans think about, isn't it?" The young officer thought about that and then replied. "No, sir. These weapons are here to defend the free countries of the Mediterranean . . . and of the Black Sea." He had said a lot in a few words; it was what we were all about.

strife, regional conflict, terrorism, the spread of deadly military technology, and the proliferation of weapons of mass destruction are all characteristics of the international system today. Unfortunately, the need for U.S. military force has not been obviated, and though the role and purpose of overseas military presence are different, presence remains an essential element in U.S. foreign and security policy.

But changes in the underlying purpose will mean changes in the context of overseas presence and in the forces that carry it out. The structure of U.S. overseas presence has already begun to change, and that change will accelerate over the next several years. The number of overseas bases will decrease rapidly, particularly as the United States withdraws forces from Europe. Reductions of U.S. forces in Europe have already halved the numbers once deployed there during the Cold War, and the U.S. Army and Air Force presence there will continue to drop dramatically. Planned withdrawals from Korea will reduce Army and Air Force presence, and as the closing of bases in the Philippines suggests, the end of the Cold War is likely to mean that fewer nations will welcome long-term U.S. military bases.

Two parallel developments are under way. As the level of U.S. overseas deployment slips downward, the percentage of naval personnel among those who remain is going up. Naval personnel currently make up less than 20 percent of the U.S. military personnel deployed overseas. Within a few years, however, that proportion may go up to roughly 50 percent. Naval forces will increasingly be seen as representatives of the entire range of U.S. military power.

The Role of Overseas Presence in the New Era

Given that U.S. overseas presence can help the transition to a new era, what does that mean in specific terms? Part of the answer lies in the utility of overseas presence to deterrence and to building coalitions.

Deterrence

The kind of deterrence we need in the new era rests on three perceptions: that the United States can intervene militarily quickly enough to undermine a fait accompli strategy; that it can intervene without incurring high casualties for our forces or the forces of our coalition partners; and that the opponent cannot split a coalition led by the United States. Overseas military presence contributes to each of these perceptions.

Some argue that the speed at which the United States can intervene does not depend on overseas deployments. Those who make this argument maintain that some military units based in the United States can deploy quickly to a crisis anywhere in the world. An extreme example of

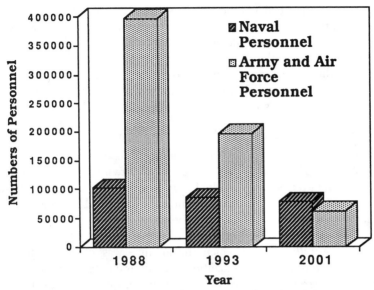

FIGURE 2:1 United States Military Personnel Deployed Overseas

this is the capacity of intercontinental ballistic missiles to strike targets thousands of miles away in less than an hour. Less extreme illustrations are the rapid-deployment capability of units such as the Army's alert airborne brigades, or the long-range-bomber forces. The former can deploy anywhere in the world within a few days, and U.S. long-range bombers can strike targets within hours of the decision to intervene militarily.

In deterrence, however, the issue is what U.S. forces the potential aggressor thinks can get there sooner rather than later. Here, the visible proximity of deployed credible U.S. forces probably has great effect, although it is hard to quantify and would vary depending on the particular situation. It seems reasonable, however, that any potential opponent of the United States contemplating a fait accompli strategy is likely to see greater risk if U.S. forces are visibly present than if they are not. Their presence does not, of course, guarantee that the United States will intervene in time to disrupt an opponent's operational scheme, but the possibility that it might appears higher and more tangible if U.S. forces are present.

Visible military presence can, of course, work against our capacity to deter a regional predator if, instead of being impressed with the invulnerability of the forces deployed overseas, the predator sees the forces as easy targets—and believes the United States also sees them that way. In that case, the threat to extract heavy U.S. casualties is worth worrying about. So, what counts in deterrence, and in the effect overseas deployments have on it, is the character of the U.S. forces we deploy. If potential predators see the forces deployed overseas as relatively invulnerable, then their visibility and ability to strike quickly works to inhibit regional aggression. If they see them as easy targets, it does not.

Alliance Maintenance and Coalition Building

It was always a problem. We had conducted exercise after exercise and spent hundreds of hours in trying to establish communications between the Sixth Fleet flagship and the various armies of our friends and allies around the Mediterranean. But it was a revelation too. I knew there was a major problem here because the future demanded that the Navy work more closely with the armies of the world. It was the armies that were tied into the governments; army generals were the most prominent military men who later became the politicians. If our Navy was going to move into a more central position so far as overseas presence in the future was concerned, we had to find a way to work with these armies—and that meant we had to be able to communicate with them.

Alliance maintenance and coalition building have potential deterrent effects, but they are valuable for other reasons also. We already have examples of how the day-to-day operating relationships within the NATO alliance help when we have to deal with situations for which the alliance was never constructed. Coalition operations during Operation Desert Storm, for example, went smoothly and efficiently largely because we and our NATO partners were familiar with how our forces could work together. The familiarity, developed over years of combined military exercises and in the daily military contact among our forces, contributed directly to the dramatic success of the coalition in the Gulf War. Obviously, without overseas presence, the kind of day-to-day interactions with our alliance partners on which we built that success could not exist. Overseas presence is the key to maintaining the benefits of alliances and adapting those benefits—and the alliances—to the demands of the new era.

Consider coalition building. Coalitions are different from alliances. They tend to be ad hoc, issue oriented, and short term and may include nations with widely divergent capabilities and interests. The fundamental fact about coalitions is that they usually are not created until the crisis that spawns them is evident.

The challenge involved with coalitions is how to set the stage in peacetime to create supporting coalitions in times of crisis.

Supporting coalitions is what we will be after. The United States does not want to build coalitions as ends in themselves or to participate in coalitions that have no clear purpose. We will have little interest in joining ones that work against our interests and foreign policies—which should go without saying, except for the tendency to use faddish terms such as coalition building so often that it is easy to lose sight of a basic fact: we want coalitions that support our policies and help us make those policies successful.

The ad hoc nature of coalitions makes this caution necessary. Unlike alliances, the members of coalitions may have little experience in working together, and coalitions can include nations normally less than friendly. Successful coalition operations face some hurdles that longer-standing alliances mitigate. They must sometimes overcome considerable distrust among their members, and they do not necessarily start from any common understanding of rules of engagement or operational familiarity. The military capabilities of coalition members can also differ greatly, and those differences can complicate and hinder effective coordination when military force has to be used.

There are two ways to overcome these problems. One is for coalitions to form around a single, clearly dominant member that, in effect, acts unilaterally in using military force. This kind of coalition is essentially demonstrative: members other than the dominant one join to signal political support for what the dominant member wants to do. The other approach is more complex. It revolves around one or a few coalition members acting to facilitate coordination among the membership. They do not dominate decisions or operations but serve as honest brokers in coalition decisions and planning and as coordinators in operations, providing common-user inputs—communications or intelligence—for all the coalition members. These two descriptions are, of course, models. Actual coalitions probably have aspects of both, although they may lean toward one or the other general type. The Desert Storm coalition, for example, tended toward the first model rather than the second.

As long as the United States is a military superpower, it will gravitate toward either the dominant member of a multilateral coalition or toward the core-coordinator role. This is probably always to our advantage, and in any case, other nations will expect it. Yet although superpower status will push the United States toward these roles, the effectiveness and skill with which we can perform them will depend greatly on the kind of groundwork we undertake before the coalition-forming crisis emerges. That is, unless we demonstrate the capacity and willingness to act responsibly as a coalition leader and partner and make other nations aware of our capacity to coordinate coalition operations, the coalitions we may wish to form, or to join, may be limited and of little use.

We were making a port call at Constanta, Romania, not too long after Ceaucescu's overthrow. The director of a local orphanage had asked if we could spare a few sailors to help with some repair work, and we had asked for volunteers. Virtually every off-duty sailor showed up at the orphanage; they all pitched in and worked long and hard. Each one left a white hat with one of the children, and each one left a little of himself. I doubt if those children will ever forget the day the Americans came. I know the sailors won't.

We should not exaggerate the extent to which U.S. military forces can do this before a coalition is formed because coalition membership is fundamentally a political decision. Two things are clear: we should try to do it, and we can do it better if we maintain an overseas military presence. Indeed, without overseas operations in peacetime, coalitions in wartime may prove unworkable. We can craft interoperability after a crisis erupts, of course, but doing so takes time, and the ability to respond quickly and effectively remains central to deterrence. Peacetime interaction—military and political—is the only way to reduce the time it takes to achieve operational coordination in a crisis. Such interaction will occur more regularly and effectively through U.S. overseas deployments.

What Naval Forces Mean to Overseas Presence

Naval forces already figure heavily in crisis response. Table 2:1, for example, traces just a few of the operations in which U.S. naval forces, often in company with other U.S. forces, have been involved over the last several years. As the table suggests, overseas presence often turns out to be significantly more than simply being there.

We should judge the utility of U.S. military overseas presence in terms that go beyond crisis response, evaluating it in terms of how the forces involved in overseas presence can also contribute to maintaining alliances, building coalitions, and supporting the bilateral relations of the United States with other nations on a day-to-day basis. U.S. military-force reductions and overseas-basing constrictions are already moving naval forces to the heart of overseas presence. This is probably an inevitable trend. It is not a bad trend because naval forces are well suited for the mission.

Naval forces operate in the air, on land, and on and under the sea. This kind of comprehensive perspective makes them of interest to foreign military establishments across the board. Naval forces have the flexibility to time their interactions with other nations, to tailor the character of those interactions, and to vary the kind of military forces involved in them. This kind of flexibility makes them particularly well suited to the demands of the new era. Consider, for example, how over-

TABLE 2:1 Naval Nonconflict Operations

Operation	Location	Dates
Counter-Narcotics Operations (monitor, interdict transport)	Caribbean, Pacific west of Latin America	Jan 1985–ongoing
FIR OPNS (challenge Libyan claims on international air space)	Mediterranean, Gulf of Sidra	Apr 1985–ongoing
SHARP EDGE (noncombatant evacuation)	Atlantic/Liberia	May 1990–Jan 1991
Maritime Interception Operations (enforce embargo on Iraq)	Red Sea and Arabian Sea	Aug 1990–ongoing
EASTERN EXIT (noncombatant evacuation)	Indian Ocean/Somalia	Jan 1991
SOUTHERN WATCH (enforce no-fly zone in Iraq)	Persian Gulf/southern Iraq	Mar 1991–ongoing
PROVIDE COMFORT (enforce no-fly zone in Iraq; provide humanitarian assistance to Kurds)	Mediterranean/northern Iraq	Apr 1991–ongoing
SEA ANGEL (humanitarian/disaster assistance to flood victims)	Bay of Bengal/Bangladesh	May–Jun 1991
FIERY VIGIL (noncombatant evacuation; humanitarian/disaster assistance to volcano victims)	Philippines	Jun 1991
ABLE MANNER (embargo of Haiti)	Caribbean	Nov 1991–ongoing
AETNA (humanitarian/disaster assistance to volcano victims)	Adriatic Sea/Sicily	Apr–May 1992
GARDEN PLOT (public-order assistance)	Los Angeles	May 1992
WATER PITCHER (humanitarian assistance)	Pacific/Micronesia	May–Jun 1992
PROVIDE PROMISE (enforce no-fly zone in Bosnia)	Adriatic/Bosnia	Jul 1992–ongoing
TYPHOON OMAR (disaster assistance)	Pacific/Guam	Aug–Sept 1992
HURRICANE ANDREW (disaster relief)	Florida	Aug–Oct 1992
RESTORE HOPE (humanitarian assistance/public-safety assistance)	Indian Ocean/Somalia	Dec 1992–ongoing

seas deployments of naval forces can play an increasingly important role in enhancing U.S. influence in what has been the keystone of alliances, the North Atlantic Treaty Organization.

In the past, U.S. authority and influence within NATO stemmed largely from the U.S. nuclear guarantee—essentially a U.S. willingness to risk strategic nuclear war with the Soviet Union in order to deter attacks on Western Europe—and the commitment of U.S. forces to defend against a massive onslaught from the East. Ground-based forces were particularly relevant in that context, and it is no coincidence that the preponderant kinds of forces the United States stationed in Europe were Army units. Nor is it surprising that, with only one exception, NATO's Supreme Allied Commander has always been a U.S. Army general.

NATO's military concerns are, however, no longer oriented against an opposing ground power. Instead, they focus increasingly on the kind of ethnic strife that convulsed Bosnia and threatens to spill out of the Balkans, and the alliance has expanded its horizons of concern beyond the geographic confines of the formal NATO-guidelines area. These new foci do not, of course, negate the importance of Army and Air Force units in maintaining U.S. influence within the alliance. They do raise the significance of the naval forces, however, that have often been selected to deal with the kind of security problems on which NATO now focuses.

There is another aspect to the reorientation within NATO. U.S. Army and Air Force presence in Europe has always been associated with extensive basing networks, embedded in the social and economic fabric of NATO's European members. In the past, this extensive land basing was a logical and necessary component of the U.S. guarantees to the alliance. Without it, the United States could not have maintained the heavy ground forces and tactical air forces needed to defend against the ground force–heavy Warsaw Treaty Organization. And without the prominent, relatively immobile Army and Air Force presence in Western Europe, the U.S. nuclear guarantee would have been questionable. The solidity and permanence of ground-force presence were precisely what was needed when the concern was how to assure our allies that we were there to help protect them from a clear and visible military threat.

Now, there is less rationale for that kind of military presence. Without a threat that justifies the use of so much valuable European real estate for U.S. bases, large-scale, permanently based U.S. military forces look increasingly anachronistic to the European (and American) public.

U.S. naval presence also depends on bases, but naval forces do not require the basing that ground units and land-based air forces do and, indeed, normally spend their operational time in international waters. As a result, their visibility to European publics is far more variable and

Aboard a Bulgarian submarine. Author, left, being briefed by captain and officer aboard Bulgarian diesel attack submarine during 1991 COMSIXTHFLEET visit to Bulgaria.

manageable. This attribute fits well with the new world era in general and with the task of managing the United States–European relationship in that new era.

The same characteristics are of use in building coalitions. Coalition building depends on the level of trust that exists between the United States and potential coalition partners before the generating crisis emerges. It is a fact of international life that most nations simply do not want foreign troops deployed more or less permanently on their territory simply to build trust. Naval forces are more logically the channel for establishing the peacetime conditions for coalition building in times of need than they are for maintaining existing alliances. As such, they become the most obvious bridge through which to mold and prepare the way for combined-force operations involving traditional alliance partners and nontraditional members.

There are a growing number of such nontraditional partners. The most obvious are the states of the former Soviet Union and other former members of the Warsaw Treaty Organization. Naval overseas presence may be the best way to establish military-to-military relationships with many of

It was the first time the United States had been invited to join the Black Sea Commanders' Conference, and I sat at the dinner table with the Turkish Chief of Naval Operations, the Commander of the Russian Black Sea Fleet, the Bulgarian Chief of Naval Operations, and the host, Admiral Anghelescu, Chief of the Romanian Navy. Anghelescu said, "We all must agree to a new relationship to maintain the security in this critical area in these very turbulent times." The Russian admiral agreed. "But," he said, "where did the Americans fit in, and when it's their turn to host the conference, where would they hold the meeting?" Anghelescu replied, "The Sixth Fleet can have the meeting in any of our countries, whenever they want. Don't we really want them here for the long term?" Even the Russian joined with the other Black Sea admirals in affirming the Romanian's point. How interesting it was, I thought, that now even former opponents saw the U.S. Navy as something that could knit their world together.

these new nations, for it is clear that they welcome contact with the United States but do not want to be smothered by it. Anything that implies a permanent, intrusive military presence by the United States is out of the question. To the extent that we want to use military-to-military contacts to help integrate these nations into the western democratic world system, naval forces look like the most effective channel for doing it.

Coalition building requires two things that are less important in alliance maintenance. One is the flexibility to take advantage of interaction opportunities that arise quickly. The other is to control overseas presence carefully—and to end it quickly if our partners need breathing room. Because these capabilities are inherent to naval forces, naval forces are inherently the best capable of coalition building.

What Overseas Presence Means to Naval Forces

Interestingly, it doesn't cost much more to deploy naval forces overseas than to keep them along the U.S. coast, for as long as the forces are operated, the difference in operations and maintenance costs boils down to what it costs to move them overseas and back to their home port. Over the last decade, it cost the United States roughly $600 million per year to operate a carrier battle group off the U.S. coast—including steaming hours, flight hours, depot maintenance, weapons expenditures, expendable stores, personnel, and readiness. It cost the United States about $50 million per year more to deploy the same force overseas, operate it there, and then return it to the United States. Fifty million dollars is nothing to ignore, but ought to be seen in perspective; it was less than 10 percent above what it cost to keep a battle group at home all the time, and less than one-tenth of one percent of the annual Navy budget.

The expanding role of naval forces in overseas presence will mean some significant changes in how those forces operate during peacetime. For one thing, naval forces will have to perform the presence role in a way that goes beyond traditional Navy-to-navy contacts. Naval forces increasingly must see themselves not only as the U.S. link to foreign navies but as the representative of the entire range of U.S. military capabilities. They will become an even more important bridge through which the United States maintains contact with foreign armies and air forces, and their mission will expand into preparing access for and facilitating the introduction of U.S. Army and Air Force units in times of need.

This will not, of course, be required of naval forces exclusively. It is unlikely that all overseas-deployed U.S. land-based units will return to the United States over the next decade, and continued multinational exercises will allow the Army and Air Force to maintain direct contact with a number of their counterpart services abroad. Given the growing prominence of naval forces, however, it would be wasteful not to use them in ways that go beyond their traditional peacetime activities. To the extent that naval forces become increasingly important as a vehicle used to build coalitions and maintain alliance ties, the need for them to cultivate direct, regular contacts with foreign armies and air forces increases also.

In many nations, armies and air forces often have more say in their nation's foreign policies than do navies. If successful coalition building depends on developing trust among foreign military establishments with regard to U.S. military capabilities and activities, then U.S. naval forces deployed overseas will have to get much more closely associated with foreign armies and air forces than has been the case in the past.

How can this be done? It is true, of course, that foreign military establishments normally welcome operations with U.S. naval forces. U.S. naval forces set the standard for naval power, a status that makes virtually all other navies interested in contact and exercises with them; to a more limited extent, non-naval foreign military establishments sense this attractiveness also. If U.S. naval forces are going to act as bridges for other U.S. military forces, however, and if they are to cultivate useful relationships with foreign military establishments, they will have to do more. While it is the inherent characteristics of flexibility, agility, and impermanence that are driving naval forces to the center of U.S. overseas military presence, their growing importance in this activity calls for changes in some of the traditional ways they have conducted operations and in the way naval forces have viewed themselves.

The notion that U.S. naval forces should serve as a bridge for other

No U.S. Marines or American amphibious ships were permitted to enter the Black Sea during the Cold War. The communists thought them too provocative; they personified power projection. Yet now, after the revolutions, the USS Whidbey Island, with three hundred marines and a platoon of U.S. Army infantry was operating there, working with Bulgarian and Romanian ground forces. This was something new—a different form of overseas presence—joint—and the Navy had brought them there. We were the bridge to armies that had once opposed us. It seemed to me to be a new model for U.S. overseas presence in an era when our forward-deployed ground forces were being pulled back.

services actually challenges what was the dominant view within the Navy for nearly three decades. Although sea lift has always been an integral part of the Navy's mission and the Navy devoted considerable resources to meeting the need to deliver other forces and their logistics support to conflicts abroad, the mainstream of U.S. naval thought emphasized combat operations by naval forces that were separate from the land campaigns that once dominated U.S. military planning. What we once called the Maritime Strategy was in many ways a modern argument in favor of the Mahanian view that the primary role of naval forces was essentially to engage other naval forces for control of the seas. The core of U.S. Cold War naval doctrine assumed relatively independent naval operations that would take place on the flanks, far from where most of the U.S. ground forces and ground-based air forces would be engaged.

Now, and in the future, U.S. naval forces must understand joint operations: in particular, how the U.S. Army and Air Force operate. The enabling function now emerging as a central component of the U.S. Navy's operational concept goes far beyond the mission of transporting U.S. forces and their supplies to a conflict; it applies also in peacetime. Indeed, the enabling function in the context of overseas presence means that the Navy, more than the other military services, must learn to operate with the other services: the Navy must understand what the other military services need to be effective in meeting their warfare tasks and assignments and what their war-fighting concepts are. This becomes an imperative because naval forces will increasingly not just represent the techniques and skills of maritime operations to foreign nations, but be required to explain the central concepts of the U.S. Army and Air Force as well. This, in turn, means operating jointly—not just conducting joint exercises from time to time.

It has implications also for the kind of naval forces the nation needs. If naval forces become a primary channel through which the entire range of U.S. military capabilities can be exercised and demonstrated in multinational operations, then they must be better able to do this. Naval forces will need platforms and communications capable of commanding and controlling large joint military operations. They will have to think much more in terms of interoperability, and they will have to tear down some of the assumptions regarding specialization that have grown up over the years. Army helicopters should operate from Navy carriers on a regular basis, supported as a matter of course by Navy logistics systems. Army tanks and vehicles should be used routinely in amphibious exercises with the Marines. Naval aviation must see itself as a component part of the full air power the nation can bring to bear on military problems, especially in support of land and air campaigns. Surface combatants and submarines must impose their defensive and offensive capabilities across the littoral and onto the land.

These orientations will anchor one end of the bridge, for to the extent that naval forces can develop a real understanding of joint operations, they can represent the range of U.S. military power abroad. But what about the other end of the bridge? How are naval forces to accomplish the overall goals of U.S. overseas military presence in deterring potential opponents, maintaining alliances, and building coalitions? The answer lies in new operational doctrine and advanced military technology.

Chapter 3

The International Significance of Advanced U.S. Military Technology

We could do it with the radar and communications capabilities of only a few U.S. Navy ships and Air Force Airborne Warning and Control aircraft. NATO wanted desperately to set up an air-defense screen throughout the entire Mediterranean, oriented southward, that could protect the sea-lanes and the littoral European nations in case any supporters of Iraq tried to launch attacks from North Africa. After several attempts to do so with the thirty to forty allied ships in the Mediterranean, our allies were amazed the U.S. could do it with only four to six ships. They quickly reorganized themselves around the American ships. We not only had an impressive air-defense capability, we also had a potent instrument of foreign policy—and there was much more in our inventory.

Operation Desert Storm, the 1991 Gulf War, confirmed a new war-fighting phenomenon. Some called it the military-technology revolution. To others it was simply the logical outcome of investments and planning that had been under way in the United States for decades. Regardless of what historians finally say, U.S. military operations in Desert Storm were a graphic demonstration of how to gain decisive combat leverage from high-technology military systems, particularly in C3I (the acronym used for command, control, communications, and intelligence), in surveillance and target acquisition, and in precision-guided, standoff munitions.

There is, of course, no single weapon or system that can claim the credit for the decisive, quick success of the air and ground campaigns in Desert Storm. But many now believe that advanced technology in these three areas enabled coalition forces to destroy Iraqi forces while sustaining so few friendly casualties. This is a new dimension to deterrence and a new means by which U.S.

military forces can help consolidate the transition to a new era. The widespread perception of a U.S. technological edge in these war-fighting areas provides the nation with a powerful instrument of foreign and security policy.[1]

THE POLITICAL LEVERAGE OF ADVANCED MILITARY TECHNOLOGY

The military utility of advanced technology is relatively straightforward, and military professionals throughout the world understand it. Advanced C3I allows U.S. commanders to work within the decision cycles of military opponents, bringing force to bear against opposing weak spots before opponents can react or prepare for the onslaught. Advanced surveillance and target acquisition—in part a function of the U.S. dominance in space, in part a reflection of the ability to process and collate vast amounts of data quickly—not only reveal an opponent's military strengths and weaknesses but allow U.S. commanders to identify and target important nodes in the opponent's command apparatus. Standoff precision-guided munitions allow U.S. forces to destroy such targets quickly, minimize the danger to our personnel, and limit collateral damage. There are also political dimensions to these capabilities as well.

The political utility of high-technology military capabilities stems from the United States's lead in C3I, surveillance and target acquisition, and precision-guided munitions. This is not to argue, of course, that only the United States will invest in the technologies that provide the edge in these areas, or that other nations have no comparable capabilities, but the lead the United States has is formidable, and those who once could challenge the U.S. superiority in these areas have either withdrawn from the competition—for example, the former Soviet Union—or are reluctant to make the investments required. The most reasonable projection is that the United States will maintain and probably increase its lead in these high-leverage capabilities over the next decade.

The underlying rhythm in mankind's long history of warfare revolves around concepts of mass and numbers. Down the centuries, victory in armed clashes has generally gone to the larger forces—particularly when the protagonists accepted and applied similar modes of conflict and military technology against each other. Yet the victories we tend to remember—the outcomes we immortalize in our poems, literature, and folk tales—highlight those instances when one of the protagonists stepped beyond the prevailing mode of combat and technology and employed something new. It was the Greek's use of subterfuge that destroyed Troy. It was the Mongol communications systems—lanterns

It was a major NATO exercise, and the two forces did not appear to be well balanced: a group composed of an American carrier and two foreign carriers, each with their supporting ships, opposed a handful of surface ships, two submarines, and some P-3 maritime-patrol aircraft. But the smaller force had some tricks in mind. We had decided to use information warfare—we would try to blunt the larger force's communications and insert misleading information into their command-and-control flow. When the exercise was over, the carrier force had lost soundly. The central importance of information warfare was manifest to all.

and banners for tactical movements, "arrow riders" for operational maneuver—that beat numerically superior Russian, Polish, Chinese, and Islamic armies. The longbows of English archers defeated the larger French army at Agincourt. The German blitzkrieg overcame larger armies in the East and the West. In all of these, the winner had an edge in new technologies and techniques—a new model of warfare that negated the opponent's numerical superiority, greater knowledge of the battlefield, or greater elan.

Today, the world is entering a new military era in which the United States has the dominant lead in the technologies and techniques that allow it to prevail against military opponents. This condition is not the result of a single technology or doctrine. It stems from the synergism among advanced communications and surveillance, computer-aided command and control, stealth, and precision weapons—and the emerging doctrine that gives the technological synergism operational potency. We do not yet agree on what to call it. To some, it represents a military technological revolution; others call it cyberwar. Whatever we ultimately call this new blend of technologies and doctrine, the United States presently monopolizes it, which gives the nation unparalleled political as well as military leverage.

Deterring Regional Predators

The U.S. technological edge can pay off in deterrence, particularly with respect to regional predators. I argued earlier that deterrence in the new era involves coping with threats to inflict high casualties on U.S. forces, and that if the United States can convince potential regional opponents its forces are invulnerable, it can undercut such threats. The key to doing this in the modern era revolves around the military weapons and systems, so effective in Desert Storm, that give the United States an edge in surveillance, intelligence, and target acquisition and in the ability to bring devastating force to bear rapidly, accurately, and at long standoff ranges.

Aegis cruiser launches standard missile. The level of technology in
the U.S. Aegis system is currently unmatched by any other nation.

Can these technologies undercut a potential opponent's threat to use
weapons of mass destruction? I think so. The direct implication of such
a threat is, of course, to inflict massive casualties. But threats to use
weapons of mass destruction also carry a more subtle message, for they
imply a willingness to cross a political threshold, thus (perhaps) stimu-
lating others elsewhere to do the same. The threat of using weapons of
mass destruction raises the prospect of high casualties as well as a
greater willingness to use such weapons throughout the world. It is a
powerful threat.

Some forms of high-technology promise to limit the casualty-produc-
ing effectiveness of such weapons. Ballistic-missile-defense systems and
long-range-strike systems, for example, can reduce the likelihood of

heavy U.S. casualties in the face of nuclear, chemical, or biological weapons. There is another way that high technology can undermine the effectiveness of threats to employ weapons of mass destruction: namely, by raising the specter of preemption. More specifically, if the United States can destroy the nuclear, chemical, or biological weapons of a potential opponent without being exposed to retaliation, threats to use weapons of mass destruction against U.S. forces in effect become potential triggers for U.S. preemptive action. Nuclear weapons, of course, provide the United States with the capability of preemptively destroying any potential regional opponent's weapons of mass destruction (if we can locate them). Yet the notion that the United States would use nuclear weapons preemptively lacks credibility on two counts: high collateral damage and the belief that our nuclear use would erode the inhibitions we seek to maintain against nuclear proliferation and nuclear use, generally.

The edge the United States has in surveillance, C3I, and precision-guided, standoff non-nuclear munitions, however, makes a U.S. threat of preemption credible. Because the United States clearly has a high interest in preventing another country from using weapons of mass destruction, its threat to destroy such weapons preemptively without resorting to nuclear weapons has deterrent significance. It would undercut the appeal to a potential predator of threatening to use weapons of mass destruction because making such threats could trigger a U.S. preemptive attack.

The U.S. edge in surveillance, C3I, and precision-guided, standoff munitions, therefore, can help the United States prevent the proliferation of weapons of mass destruction. By undercutting an opponent's interest in threatening to use weapons of mass destruction, it devalues having such weapons. By degrading the value of weapons of mass destruction, the engine that drives the proliferation of such weapons may start to run out of fuel.

Alliance Maintenance

The technological edge can also help the United States maintain its alliance leadership. This is because the U.S. superiority in these areas can generate the same kind of political leverage we once had from our nuclear capabilities, which are now essentially irrelevant so far as alliance politics are concerned. For nearly five decades the U.S.-European security relationship rested on a formal U.S. commitment to risk nuclear war to deter a Soviet attack on Europe. As the West's nuclear superpower, the United States had preeminent authority within the NATO alliance to organize and direct Western European defenses. With the collapse of the Soviet Union, however, the nuclear rationale for

U.S. dominance within the alliance also collapsed, and with it, by extension, much of the influence the United States had in European affairs. To maintain influence with our allies, therefore, we have to find a substitute for the nuclear umbrella and shift our relationship with our allies from the old Cold War role of dominant partner to one that is more complementary in the new era.

We can base that new relationship on the U.S. technological edge in C3I, surveillance and target acquisition, and precision-guided munitions. These are high-leverage capabilities, attractive to all nations, but very costly to develop; to get the benefit of such capabilities while avoiding their cost, working with the United States becomes an appealing option to other nations. This could give the United States some say in what our allies plan to do with their forces. This new relationship is potentially uncomfortable, however—we may be reluctant to give up our historical dominance of the alliance, and our allies may be reluctant to depend on the high-tech supplements from U.S. forces.

Yet this new relationship would appeal to our European allies because it replaces the dependency they once had on the United States for their survival, with an interdependency that stems from the utility, cost avoidance, and lifesaving benefits of working with the United States in pursuit of their foreign and security goals. This is a more stable and healthier relationship than existed during the Cold War when U.S. nuclear capabilities so dominated the NATO relationship that it was hard for the Europeans to feel anything but subordinate; they were partners in the alliance, to be sure, but clearly junior partners. The proposed new relationship promises to be a more equal partnership, more complementary, and one far more consistent with the world as it now exists.

It may seem paradoxical to argue that the United States, having become the world's only superpower, should now seek to elevate the military influence and capabilities of its allies. It is precisely because there is no longer another superpower to threaten them, however, that our allies want greater independence and flexibility. Similarly, it is because the threat that dominated the Cold War is gone that the United States must seek other ways of maintaining U.S. leadership in NATO and our other alliances.

THE ROLE OF NAVAL FORCES

High-technology military capabilities must be visible to have the kind of political utility sketched above, and although all forward-deployed U.S. military forces employ and benefit from the kind of military technologies discussed above, forward-deployed naval forces—for several reasons—may be the best means of demonstrating them.

The mobility of naval forces allows them to demonstrate these capabilities to the leadership of any country that borders the sea. They have the flexibility and agility to move to crisis areas before hostilities begin. They can stay there, visible and close enough to intervene immediately if necessary, for as long as the tension continues, without irrevocably committing U.S. forces on the ground. They can establish and maintain the sort of local military presence that is useful in this new era of deterrence. Other U.S. force components can also do this, but it normally requires basing in the area, basing that may become available only after hostilities begin.

Naval forces have some other attributes that make them logical choices as vehicles for generating political leverage from the U.S. high-technology edge. While the U.S. Army and Air Force have important technical edges over their foreign counterparts, the U.S. edge in naval capabilities is the most pronounced. This means the attraction to foreign militaries of working with the U.S. Navy is relatively high, for the greater the edge in military technology, the more interest foreign military counterparts have in working with that force component, in part to learn about the technologies in which they lag, in part to gain operational supplements to their own military capabilities. U.S. naval forces, as a result, are the most logical and attractive bridges to foreign militaries because of this edge in high-leverage technologies. Of all the U.S. force components, they are the most capable of enhancing the capabilities of their foreign counterparts.

To the extent we allow other naval forces to tie into the capabilities brought to bear by U.S. naval forces, their own reach and capacity to coordinate joint operations will expand dramatically. This is of use not only to other navies. Indeed, to the extent the United States can use its naval force C3I capabilities to supplement allied ground-force capabilities, it is likely to enhance U.S. political influence.

IMPLICATIONS FOR U.S. NAVAL FORCES

Having these new capabilities is the foundation for deriving political leverage. To achieve their deterrence potential and the kind of alliance and coalition cohesion these capabilities promise, however, we must demonstrate them. Other nations have to understand what U.S. naval forces will be able to do if we are to derive the full benefits of our technological edge. Fortunately, the United States has recent experience in demonstrating the political utility of high-technology naval capabilities.

Over the last several years, for example, the U.S. Sixth Fleet has worked with allied navies and air forces in a number of ways that use American military technology to enhance allied capabilities. By establishing satellite communications links between Spanish ships and U.S.

broad-area surveillance assets in the Mediterranean, Spanish antisubmarine-warfare forces suddenly became capable of what were, for the Spanish, true breakthroughs in contacting and prosecuting underwater targets. By linking allied communications with those of the U.S. Navy, the range of allied sea and air operations more than quadrupled. By working with U.S. Maritime Action Groups, and tying into the area surveillance and communications capabilities brought by the maritime action groups, the area of influence for the major carrier and surface components of the French, Spanish, and Italian navies suddenly expanded far beyond anything these forces had experienced. The C3I and surveillance assets of U.S. forces held together the multinational coalition of naval forces off the Balkan coast.

Experience suggests strongly that NATO navies and other forces like to work with U.S. forces not only because doing so affords them a chance to exercise with U.S. technology but also because it allows them to employ their own forces more effectively. The Navy should, of course, continue to encourage multinational participation in such exercises. To maximize the political leverage the United States can derive from its military technology, however, we should adjust some of the exercise procedures and arrangements that now exist.

More extensive, regular contact between U.S. naval forces and the armies and air forces of foreign nations is called for because of their relatively greater impact on the defense and foreign policies of their nations. If U.S. naval forces are to play a greater role in demonstrating U.S. military advanced technology, contacts that go beyond Navy-to-navy interactions will expand the political leverage we hope to get through such demonstrations. The increasing ability of naval air and sea vessels to link with such systems as the joint surveillance and targeting system (JSTARS) and the airborne warning and control system (AWACS), for example, promises not only better war-fighting capability on the part of U.S. naval forces—particularly in the complex electromagnetic environment of the littoral and over land—but dictates an increased capacity for those naval forces to link the surveillance capabilities of such systems to foreign armed forces.

THEATER BALLISTIC-MISSILE DEFENSES: THE ROLE OF TECHNOLOGY IN U.S. INTERNATIONAL RELATIONS

Most of the discussion in this chapter has been rather general, and I would like to provide a more precise illustration of the role of high technology in international affairs by discussing U.S. theater ballistic-missile defenses, a particularly promising example of American advanced military technology.

Twenty years ago, during the 1973 Arab-Israeli War, Egyptian forces launched the first Scud ballistic missile used in combat. In the 1980s the Iranians and Iraqis fired more than six hundred similar ballistic missiles at each other's cities. In the late 1980s the Soviet-supplied Afghan Army launched more than two thousand Scuds against Mujaheddin bases, and Iraq, during the 1991 Gulf War, fired nearly one hundred ballistic missiles at targets up to six hundred kilometers away in Israel and Saudi Arabia. The twentieth century almost certainly will end without the kind of strategic nuclear-ballistic-missile war that so dominated national security concerns for the last half of the century. But we have seen the harbinger of another specter—a proliferation of theater ballistic missiles, at least some armed with weapons of mass destruction (chemical, biological, or nuclear), in the hands of governments who appear ready to use them against opponents.

Ballistic-Missile Proliferation

How real is ballistic-missile proliferation, and what is its military and political significance? The number of long-range ballistic missiles capable of striking the United States is going down, not up. Strategic-arms treaties and other factors will result in major decreases in such missiles, and there will probably be few new members of the "ICBM club" for at least a decade. The missile proliferation that is of concern, then, involves ballistic missiles with ranges of about six hundred nautical miles (one thousand kilometers). These are generically called theater ballistic missiles because they are capable of reaching targets in neighboring nations or within the same geographical region. The overall trends regarding these kinds of missiles are less heartening. Their numbers have been increasing in areas of the world where international tensions remain high, more nations are acquiring them, and the missiles' accuracy and reliability are improving.

The proliferation of ballistic missiles is not automatic; there are pressures working against it, and the rate at which it occurs varies. Still, strong engines drive missile proliferation. Nations acquire them for a number of reasons: to offset missiles acquired by neighbors, to gain internal and international prestige, and to compete in the global aerospace and weapons-systems marketplace. They do it because the missiles provide an offensive military capability at far less expense than does a fleet of modern tactical attack aircraft.

Thus far, the ballistic missiles used in combat have not been militarily effective. Their use in the Iran-Iraq war probably killed hundreds of civilians but did not shift the military balance between those two nations, nor degrade the military effectiveness of the forces that confronted each other. Their use in Afghanistan did not turn the military tide. Their use in the Gulf War did not affect the outcome of Operation Desert Storm. The perception that these are not militarily effective weapons, however, could change.

Ballistic Missile–Tactical Aircraft Trade-Offs

Most of the nations with these missiles also have strike aircraft, and there are some trade-offs. Both have similar ranges. Aircraft-delivered ordnance is more accurate than the ballistic missiles now being acquired by Iran, Israel, Egypt, Syria, India, Pakistan, North Korea, Taiwan, and others. Aircraft can be used more than once. But mobile missiles have greater prelaunch survivability, are far easier to produce indigenously, and, as table 3:1 suggests, are cheaper to buy.

Until recently, planners favored manned aircraft for long-range tactical strikes. Over the last five years, however, developing nations have tended to reduce their numbers of combat aircraft while increasing their arsenal of ballistic missiles, partly because the unit costs of modern aircraft are increasing while the costs of ballistic missiles are going down. When the full costs of supporting and maintaining a manned-aircraft capability are included, the relatively lower costs associated with ballistic missiles become increasingly obvious.

Part of the reason for the growing interest in missiles may be more ominous. From a military point of view, acquiring ballistic missiles makes the most sense when paralleled by an intention to use them to deliver nuclear weapons. Virtually all trade-off analyses of the cost effectiveness of aircraft and missiles reach the same conclusion: missiles are dramatically more cost effective in delivering nuclear weapons. Decreased accuracy is acceptable when nuclear weapons are involved.

To deliver conventional explosives or chemical weapons, accuracy is more important, and aircraft emerge as the better buy. Assessments of how many conventionally armed Iraqi Scud missiles it would have taken to destroy the port facilities of Dhahran during the Gulf War end up

TABLE 3:1 Foreign Military Purchase Options: 1985 and 1994

$50 Million . . .

Could buy in 1985	Can buy today
6 Su-24 aircraft, or	1 MiG-29 aircraft, or
2.3 Mirage IV aircraft, or	2 Mirage 2000 aircraft, or
2.6 F-5 aircraft, or	1.3 F-16 aircraft, or
3 fifteen-man terrorist cells, or	3 fifteen-man terrorist cells, or
32 Scud B ballistic missiles	48 Scud B ballistic missiles, or
	16 Chinese M-9 ballistic missiles

with estimates in the hundreds. The accuracy of the Iraqi missiles was so poor that Iraq probably could not have destroyed the facilities even if it had used its entire missile inventory in the attempt and there had been no Patriot defense systems in theater. Aircraft always have turned out to be far more cost effective in such analyses, particularly when those analyses consider historical data regarding aircraft attrition.

Nuclear weapons, however, change these kinds of judgments; the destructive potential of a nuclear weapon more than balances the effects of higher mission reliability and delivery accuracy of aircraft. It takes no fancy analytic techniques to come up with what intuitively makes sense, and any regional power that considers the pros and cons of ballistic missiles versus aircraft will opt for the missiles if it intends to arm them with nuclear weapons.

Likewise, Desert Storm altered to some degree the conclusion that aircraft are the most cost-effective means of acquiring a longer-range non-nuclear offensive capability, for it suggested that modern U.S. air defenses and offensive counter-air capabilities are so formidable that the probability of opposing aircraft successfully delivering large amounts of ordnance over a sustained campaign are low. Most of the Iraqi air force was destroyed on the ground or shot down when it could not escape. No Iraqi aircraft successfully attacked coalition forces. Future regional opponents might argue, of course, that their air operations against U.S. forces would be different and effective. But hubris aside, any potential opponent contemplating fighting the United States after Desert Storm may now see ballistic missiles as a much more cost-effective means of attacking U.S. forces, or the base facilities they would use, even if the missiles carry non-nuclear warheads. After all, more American servicemen were killed by a single Iraqi missile than by the entire Iraqi air force.

Whether these considerations will lead regional predators to use theater ballistic missiles as counters to U.S. military power, or push them into trying to arm their missiles with nuclear weapons, remains to be seen. The inaccuracy of the ballistic missiles currently fielded by possible opponents certainly does not mean the U.S. military can ignore them. Practically speaking, the nation will not countenance sending its military men and women into harm's way without counters to such missiles. Thus, while current theater-ballistic-missile technology is not a war stopper, reducing the threat it constitutes is a military imperative.

The Political Impact of Theater Ballistic Missiles

While theater ballistic missiles have not yet demonstrated much military effectiveness, their appeal to the nations acquiring them probably has relatively little to do with whatever military potential they have anyway. From the time the first German V-2 burst in the United Kingdom until the

Iraqi-modified Scuds streaked into Israel and Saudi Arabia, nations have used theater ballistic missiles as terror weapons and have aimed them not at military forces but at civilian populations. Even if they are eventually armed with nuclear warheads, the political, psychological, and international import of such weapons would probably overshadow their military significance. We must consider the politics of theater ballistic missiles, for it is those which are driving missile proliferation. The political dynamics must be understood and neutralized if the United States is going to stop the spread of these weapons, deter their use, and turn the political dynamics to our own strategic and international benefit.

Theater Ballistic Missiles and Regime Authority

Consider the prestige theater ballistic missiles convey to their owners. When authoritarian leaders parade their ballistic missiles, as Saddam Hussein did, they are trying to impress the international community. But they also are interested in internal audiences, for missiles are symbols of the regime's power over internal opponents. This is true even though, with the exception of the Afghan civil war, ballistic missiles have not been used against internal enemies, which authoritarian regimes almost always characterize as agents of external powers. (Since Saddam Hussein, by his own admission, is the "great leader of all the Iraqi people," those Iraqis who oppose him simply cannot be true Iraqis but must represent the sinister intentions of outsiders. Lin Piao turned out to be a "Russian agent" after his opposition to Mao Tse-tung surfaced. Deng Shao-ping, at least while he was in prison, was a capitalist spy.)

Linking internal and external enemies converts the display of weapons that can strike out against foreign powers—usually in the same region—into statements of the regime's internal authority, in effect proclaiming that the regime can punish and destroy the foreign masters and supporters of those inside who challenge the regime's authority. The prime message of parades featuring theater ballistic missiles is intended for internal opposition groups and is straightforward: "I can crush you, punish your foreign supporters, and deter them from sending replacements. Your opposition is doomed."

However useful such displays may be in supplementing the other means authoritarian regimes have to maintain their rule, they also demonstrate a potential political weakness. Having linked their internal authority to symbols of international potency, if their subjects see those symbols as impotent, the regime's authority erodes. This does not mean, of course, that theater-ballistic-missile defenses spell the end to authoritarian regimes. But it does point to one of the ways effective defenses can have political effects. They can neutralize and counter one of the sources of an authoritarian regime's power within its domain.

Theater Ballistic Missiles and Base Access

Ballistic missiles also have international implications. Even if potential regional opponents of the United States recognize the military limitations of their missiles, they may see them as the means of denying U.S. access to bases in the region. As terror weapons, ballistic missiles offer a nation a kind of deterrence, not against the United States, perhaps, but against other nations in the region that by granting base access to U.S. forces would allow the United States to bring decisive military power to bear. Threatening to attack population centers in those neighboring countries if they allow U.S. or U.S.-led coalitions to use their territory may not prevent them from doing so—but the neighboring countries cannot ignore such threats.

Powerful naval forces and long-range aircraft, both of which may alleviate the need for extensive land bases, obviously undercut such threats, but mounting major military operations without regional basing access is not easy. We know that—and so do potential regional predators.

A defensive shield that can undercut threats to attack regional nations if they allow base access to U.S. or coalition forces is, therefore, obviously useful in such scenarios. But there is a nuance to this kind of situation that bears noting: threatening ballistic-missile attack if a neighboring country offers U.S. forces base access is different from threatening those attacks because base access was provided. In the first case, defensive systems that require base access cannot help those nations that worry about the threat; in the second case, they may be able to help.

Nations facing the threat of ballistic-missile attacks if they grant access must believe either that the threat is a bluff or that they can mount effective defenses against it. This situation is more likely to result in the denial of basing access than the second case, when defenses are likely to be in place. It is the difference between deterring an action that has not yet been taken and reversing something that has already been done. The history of international relations suggests the first is easier to accomplish with threats than the second. The implication is, of course, that a ballistic-missile-defense system that does not require base access undercuts threats designed to deny access better than one that requires what the opponent is trying to deny.

Theater Ballistic Missiles and Coalition Solidarity

Base access is one expression of a successful coalition. There are others, including combined military operations, financial support for the operations, and coordinated economic embargoes. Aggressors might threaten theater-ballistic-missile attacks to undercut each of the things an opposing coalition may try to bring to bear against them and to divide coalition members. Would the coalition members be as willing to commit their military personnel in combined operations without any defenses? Perhaps, since they would understand the military limitations of the kind of theater ballistic missiles they faced. But would they be willing to risk committing forces and suffering the economic effects of ballistic-missile attacks on facilities that provided oil or other natural resources to their economies? The point is not that theater ballistic missiles are necessarily coalition breakers. It is that lack of defenses against them can make building and maintaining coalitions more difficult.

The obverse is probably true. The ability of the United States to defend against theater-ballistic-missile attacks gives it a natural leadership position in any multilateral coalition facing the threat of ballistic missiles. Indeed, theater-ballistic-missile defenses are probably the best example of how the high-technology military capabilities of the United States can help the United States internationally. The United States has quite an edge in the capacity to field theater-ballistic-missile defenses. Few, if any, nations are likely to commit the resources required to match that capability. If threats of theater-ballistic-missile attacks grow in international relations, the leverage the United States has in international relations can also increase because it will have the only capability to undercut those threats.

Theater Ballistic Missiles and Regional Arms Races

Ballistic-missile defenses may also figure in the tendency of regional opponents to acquire theater ballistic missiles to offset similar missiles acquired by their regional rivals. Some explain it as a regional variation of the action-reaction process that once helped fuel the strategic-arms race between the United States and the Soviet Union. Rivalries stimulate ballistic-missile arms races and the tensions that accompany such races. More recently, the effort by Israel, and perhaps other nations, to develop their own antiballistic-missile systems may drive the action-reaction process up a notch and stimulate rivals to try to acquire the kinds of theater ballistic missiles that can penetrate defenses.

Ballistic-missile proliferation is not in the U.S. interest. It adds to regional tensions, increases the possibility of threats and counterthreats, and fuels the search for ever-deadlier missile systems. The capacity of the United States to extend ballistic-missile defenses across vast areas is, then, a potential aid in the nation's efforts to stem these trends. It is in some ways analogous to the effects of the nuclear umbrella in the Cold War. The nuclear guarantee by the United States not only welded together the alliances in which the United States was a member and made U.S. leadership inevitable, but helped deter many nations, which had the capability to develop nuclear weapons, from doing so.

The Political Leverage of Sea-Based TBMD

I think that sea-based theater-ballistic-missile defenses have some particular advantages in the political context. The decreased need for base access on the part of sea-based systems, for example, could undercut threats by regional antagonists to attack nearby neighbors that offer basing to U.S. forces. Sea-based defenses are not inherently better than land-based systems, but in some cases they may be the only way to get a capability in place. A nation that can benefit from a sea-based missile defense without first granting base rights may later be willing to allow U.S. forces to come ashore. Sea-based theater-ballistic-missile defenses may turn out to be one of the best examples of how naval forces can enable the application of joint military force, for they may be the key to the kind of regional base access on which it depends.

Sea-based ballistic-missile defenses also may turn out to be one of the best instruments the United States has to maintain its leadership in alliances and multilateral coalitions. As U.S. land-based forces come home, U.S. naval forces will increasingly become the bridge connecting the United States with other nations in military and security issues. The ability to offer effective defenses can link the U.S. Navy not only with the naval forces of other nations—whose mobility largely frees them from worrying about theater-ballistic-missile attacks—but also with the armies and land-based air forces of those nations, which do have to worry.

Sea-based theater-missile defenses, then, should be considered not only in military terms, in which their mobility and flexibility figure heavily, but in their political payoff. They are a prime example of the way advanced military technology with overseas naval forces can provide the kind of deterrence, alliance maintenance, and coalition building the new era calls for.

In summary, I believe the U.S. lead in the military technological revolution can become a major contributor to U.S. foreign policy in this new era, both in a negative sense—it can become the basis for deterrence—and in an affirmative sense by providing our friends advantages they could not easily acquire by themselves.

Ballistic-missile defenses illustrate the general point, but they are not the only manifestation of how our lead in the military technical revolution can provide political leverage. We have a clearly superior capacity to tie together intelligence and strike planning and, when these are coupled with the emerging systems of standoff weapons, will be able to focus a precise strategic attack on an enemy with up to five hundred coordinated and well-timed, long-range conventional missiles without risking the lives of pilots or the threat of prisoners of war. This is a disproportionate capability compared to what our potential opponents and our potential coalition partners will have any time soon. We will also have an edge in the capacity to affect the battlefield and troop movements over land. We are developing this capacity through a system of remotely piloted vehicles and national surveillance assets, which, when coupled with the ability to attack directly from the sea using sensor-fused standoff weapons, such as the Joint Standoff Weapon (JSOW) and the Army Tactical Missile System (ATACMS), will be able to disrupt virtually any opponent's ground-force operations. Together, the battlefield dominance, long-range strategic strike (with conventional standoff missiles), and theater-ballistic-missile defenses will give the United States a decisive military capacity.

The issue that remains is how these capabilities can be integrated into U.S. foreign policy.

Chapter 4

Political-Military Coordination

It happened during a port visit to Bulgaria. Bulgarian President Zhelev had called me to Sofia, and now the U.S. Ambassador and I were being ushered into the president's office. After the normal welcoming formalities, Zhelev turned to me and said he had a request. "I want you to tell NATO and the President of the United States," he said, "that Bulgaria wants to join NATO. I can think of no better official to present this request than the commander of the U.S. Sixth Fleet." I informed President Zhelev that this matter was way above my pay grade but that I would, of course, report our conversation to the U.S. government and to NATO headquarters. As I tried to step carefully through this delicate issue of protocol and diplomacy, it struck me that the new era of political-military coordination was already in full swing.

This chapter focuses on the relationship between U.S. military forces and the policy-diplomatic structure through which the United States deals with the world. The phrase "policy-diplomatic structure" refers to the offices in Washington that set foreign policy and the network of U.S. diplomatic missions abroad and overseas military commands that implement those policies. Together, this is an immense structure, for it includes not only the State and Defense Department bureaucracies but also much of the intelligence community, many of the committees in Congress, parts of the Agriculture, Treasury, and Commerce Departments, and a wide range of coordinating mechanisms in Washington and throughout the world.

This network is part of the context of the new era in which naval forces will operate, but it is more than just a backdrop, for it acts as the interface between U.S. military forces and the external world, ultimately directing U.S. military activity overseas and explaining that activity to other nations. It is the structure we will use to test the nascent theories of deterrence, alliance maintenance, and coalition building—or it can prevent such tests.

Although U.S. military and diplomatic actions have always been coordinated, the structures through which this happens are rooted in the Cold War. Unfortunately, the current patterns of military-diplomatic interaction still reflect the old era. The nation should centralize and streamline its mechanisms for formulating and coordinating regional foreign and security policies. It also needs closer and different kinds of coordination between U.S. diplomatic representatives and the U.S. military commanders abroad.

THE LEGACY OF THE OLD ERA

If you look at how the United States develops and implements its foreign policies, the complexity and rigidity of the current procedures and mechanisms are striking. This is not surprising. U.S. diplomatic-military interactions, devoted primarily to containing Soviet expansion and deterring Soviet attack, grew since the late 1940s under essentially the same national policy of containment. The magnitude of this task, which persisted for decades, required the efforts of a host of people; a tremendous expansion of offices, missions, commands, and committees paralleled their efforts. By 1990, the formulation and management of U.S. foreign and security policy was one of the world's largest enterprises.

It is interesting to compare the size and bureaucratic complexity of that enterprise today with the relatively Spartan, streamlined, and centralized policy-making structure that existed at the birth of the containment policy. Take an organizational chart of the State Department in 1947 and lay it next to today's, or count the separate offices in the War Department of 1947 that had something to do with foreign policy and compare it with the number of current Defense Department offices that perform analogous functions, or read the memoirs of Harry Truman, Dean Acheson, or George Marshall where they touch on the governmental structure through which they orchestrated military and diplomatic actions. The contrasts are striking. Somehow the architects of the policy framework that set the parameters for the following four decades were able to define this national consensus and get it implemented without the complex plethora of offices, committees, and agencies that exist today. Maybe that is the reason they could.

Despite the complexity of the mechanisms that coordinate the nation's military and foreign policies, and despite the almost steady growth in the numbers of people involved in the endeavor, there is a remarkable rigidity to the undertaking. Following established procedures and routine have often become an end in themselves. I make this observation not as a criticism, for there were important reasons for elevating procedural considerations during the Cold War. The stakes were

We had coordinated it carefully, for it was to be the first multinational naval exercise in the Black Sea that involved elements of the Sixth Fleet, the Russian Black Sea Fleet, and the Bulgarian and Romanian navies. The Black Sea nations that were to be involved had worked hard on the idea, too, investing considerable political capital on the idea. Then, forty-eight hours before the exercise was to begin, a fourth-level State Department bureaucrat directed the U.S. ambassador to turn it off. We later found out that higher levels had never approved canceling the exercise. The work and political face had been lost, though—a strange way, I thought, for the nation to run its diplomacy.

high, for if the confrontation between East and West had ever degenerated into a direct military conflict, the world could have been destroyed. Because of such stakes, virtually all other nations, and particularly those in Europe, saw great value in making the actions of their superpower ally as predictable as possible. Procedure was the only substitute they had for raw power.

The global network of institutions that grew from the superpower confrontation was functional in the bipolar world because everyone in the world had a stake in assuring the confrontation did not come to military blows. NATO during the Cold War was an instrument through which the West combined its strengths and extended the American nuclear deterrent beyond the shores of the United States. From the standpoint of its European members, however, it was also a mechanism through which its European members could influence, channel, and control the actions of the United States vis-à-vis the Soviet Union. The United States understood this, accepted it, and worked with allies under the terms of the alliance, which stressed predictable, familiar procedures.

In time, the emphasis on procedure and regularity calcified the channels through which U.S. foreign and military policy was implemented, and it conditioned what could be done quickly. Whatever the benefits of the system that grew up within the context of containment and the bipolar world, that system now has a number of aspects whose utility in the new era is questionable:

—Elaborate alliance-consultation mechanisms and planning procedures, as in NATO, can cause up to a two-year lead time to schedule military exercises among the allies.
—Scheduled exercises between U.S. and foreign military forces still must be vetted, one-by-one, with the State Department and National Security Council as their start date approaches.
—The rigid separation of funds between the Defense Budget and the Foreign Assistance Budget has prevented the Secretary of Defense, the

Joint Chiefs of Staff, and the unified commanders from using defense funds for foreign activities and assistance. Small funds for these purposes were established in 1987, but the amounts involved are too minuscule to allow much impact.

—Unified commanders with areas of operational responsibility abroad have no representatives of their own who can communicate directly with the military in foreign countries without clearance by the U.S. ambassador. Tradition restricts what military attachés do (they are part of the intelligence community and are not under the supervision of the unified commanders), and the law restricts security-assistance officers to administering security-assistance programs. There is nothing wrong with the idea of U.S. ambassadors controlling contact between the U.S. military and other nations in peacetime, but there is no regional or country-by-country, day-to-day, military-to-ambassadorial planning or policy mechanism for optimal use of U.S. military forces in the region. We have no coordinated structure to use U.S. military forces in a region for the maximum benefit of the U.S. national interest, political, economic, and military.

—Hierarchical, top-heavy U.S. command structures often limit the extent to which U.S. forces at the operational level can work together with one another or with the U.S. diplomatic structure. To integrate day-to-day training with the U.S. Army V Corps commander, for example, the U.S. Sixth Fleet commander must clear contact with his operational counterpart through the admiral who serves as Commander in Chief, U.S. Navy, Europe; who must clear such requests with his superior, the U.S. general who commands all U.S. forces in Europe, before approaching his four-star counterpart, the general who commands U.S. Army forces assigned to Europe. If this chain of headquarters agrees, the Sixth Fleet and V Corps commanders can talk to each other about joint training exercises or other matters of mutual interest. By this time the exercise opportunity may have passed. Contact between the U.S. diplomatic structure and the operational level of the U.S. forces deployed overseas is similarly convoluted and hardly conducive to easy dialogue about how U.S. forces deployed overseas can facilitate U.S. foreign-policy-goal achievement.

The issue here is not whether bureaucratic mechanisms are needed to coordinate and integrate political-military policy-making and implementation. They are and always will be. The real issue is how those that grew up during the Cold War ought to be altered to meet the demands of the new era and the problems it generates.

What kind of structure and procedures do we need now, when the old policy of containment is being replaced by the new, trifurcated problem of deterring regional predators, redirecting alliances, and building new coalitions? We will work out the complete answer in practice over the next several years, but the right path is already visible.

POLICY-MAKING IN WASHINGTON

The fundamental problem with political-military policy-making in the nation's capital is its fractionated character. Political-military interactions are viewed as virtually every office's responsibility, and policy-making reflects everyone's input. Because every office participates in devising the policy, the policies themselves are slow in evolving and usually turn out to be so general when they ultimately emerge that they are not useful guides to the institutions and agencies abroad charged with implementing them. This promotes the kind of daily flow of communications and clarifying instructions between Washington and its governmental and military extensions overseas that some have pointed to as micromanagement. The technology of modern communications makes this possible, but the reason it occurs goes deeper than the technological capacity to do it.

The system worked in the past largely because the basic policy of containment provided a common set of assumptions that all the policy-making participants carried into the meetings, discussions, and debates that are the government's way of life in Washington. Despite the amazing number of hours spent in making policy in Washington, the legions of officials and their staffs involved dealt with what were marginal and incremental proposals for change. The participants all worked from the same blueprint, and there was a premium on avoiding radical shifts in political-military policy. Maintaining the alliances we built to help contain the Soviet Union depended on consensus, convoluted procedures, and, above all, the avoidance of precipitous changes. Widespread participation in policy-making in Washington and the fuzzy boundaries between policy-making and policy implementation were functional because they tended to rule out sudden shifts in policy and experimentation.

Now, however, there is no conceptual umbrella that serves as a common starting point for internal policy discussion the way the broad goal of containment did, and the frame of reference for political-military policy-making has shifted from a global to a regional context. The absence of a common blueprint for policy-making and the regional focus unleash the constraints on parochial and disparate views and interests within the government. This, in turn, can change the policy process in Washington from one that produced slow, incremental policy evolution to one that is for all intents and purposes gridlocked and unable to produce any coherent policy at all.

Author, center, with the two Secretaries of Defense he served as senior military assistant, Secretary Richard Cheney (left) and Secretary Frank Carlucci (right).

The path to policy-making that fits the new era's demand for new flexibility, experimentation, and change, therefore, points toward streamlining the process and moving toward more focus in Washington, with the authority and responsibility for regional policy-making narrowed to fewer participants.

Specifically, we should clearly identify offices at the undersecretary level in the State and Defense Departments as centers for policy-making with regard to how the regional military and diplomatic institutions abroad are to work together in the new era. It is true that the Undersecretary of Defense for Policy and the Undersecretary of State for International Security imply that this kind of centralization is already in place. Yet the official titles tend to hide the fact that a number of other offices believe they are charged with political-military policy-making and act as if they were. Each of the regional bureaus in the State Department, the elements of the National Security Council staff, divisions within the Joint Chiefs of Staff Office, other offices in the Secretary of Defense's office, the Defense Security Assistance Agency, and others currently claim seats at any policy discussion of how diplomatic and military policy should be integrated. Until we streamline the process, they would all be correct in their claims for access.

We should consolidate the policy-making authority and responsibility in a smaller number of offices at the undersecretary level—a partnership between the Defense Department as a whole and the State Department, perhaps oriented region by region, with crisp political-military decisions (especially lower-level ones) and communications with the unified commanders in chief and ambassadors.

POLICY IMPLEMENTATION OVERSEAS

Beneath the complexity of the offices, bureaus, and coordinating committees through which the nation melds its military and foreign policies in Washington lies a basic asymmetry in the military and diplomatic chains of authority through which those policies are implemented. On the military side, the chain of command runs from the Secretary of Defense to unified military commanders with specific geographical areas of responsibility. The Commander in Chief, Pacific, for example, has an operational responsibility for nearly 70 percent of the earth's water area—some one hundred million square miles—and a total land area of more than ten million square miles. The U.S. Central Command's area of responsibility stretches from Egypt to Pakistan, and from the southern border of Kenya to the Russian-Iranian frontier. The U.S. European Command includes about four million square miles of Europe; the U.S. Atlantic Command has planning and military operational responsibilities for an ocean area of about thirty-two million square miles. In some cases, the military chain of command extends into what can be thought of as military subregions. The Sixth Fleet, for example, normally operates in the Mediterranean with an operational purview that includes all the nations that border that body of water.

The military chain through which political-military policy is normally implemented, however, does not extend into individual nations in the sense of having operational responsibilities defined by another nation's boundaries. There are exceptions to this; the responsibilities of U.S. forces stationed in South Korea are probably the best example. The U.S. military units or detachments stationed in foreign nations are, however, normally assigned specifically limited missions and responsibilities. In effect, the U.S. military chain of command ends at the regional or subregional level.

In contrast, the U.S. diplomatic chain generally extends from Washington directly to U.S. missions in the individual foreign nation, without any regional or subregional structure that parallels the military chain. There are exceptions to this pattern, but unlike the military chain

In 1990 one of the principal leaders of Yugoslavia contacted me directly. I had never met him, and I was surprised that he wanted direct talks with a foreign fleet commander. The message he brought was straightforward and chilling: "We Yugoslavians request the presence of the U.S. Sixth Fleet in any way possible. This will be the last chance to help." I sent the message through the normal channels to the State Department, and days later the system responded. We were told not to do anything with regard to Yugoslavia, nor enter the Adriatic. It was the last chance, indeed, and I have often wondered whether the Sixth Fleet might have made a difference in Yugoslavia's tragedy.

of command, the diplomatic chain of authority normally extends directly from a regional bureau within the State Department in Washington to the country level.

This asymmetry limits the ease with which political-military policy can be implemented overseas. The military side of the equation is regionally oriented and managed inside the region; the diplomatic side focuses on individual nations and is managed from Washington. This does not, of course, prevent the regional or subregional military commander from working with the heads of the U.S. diplomatic missions assigned to individual foreign nations. Yet the structural asymmetry tends to work against this cooperation so that it normally occurs only in response to a specific policy or action that emanates from Washington. There is no one in the diplomatic chain with whom the military regional commander can talk as a bureaucratic peer, and normally no senior U.S. military representative with whom a U.S. ambassador can deal at the country level. All of this inhibits the individuals in the military and diplomatic chains of command from working together either to formulate policy recommendations or to experiment with and explore new ways of integrating U.S. foreign diplomatic and military policy at the regional or the individual country level.

It also accounts for the lack of awareness on the part of the members of one chain of command—either the military or the diplomatic—for the concerns of the members of the other chain. Members of the diplomatic chain may have a general understanding of military operations and capabilities, but this is more often garnered from their personal military service. Members of the military chain may also have a general working understanding of American diplomacy but usually have little in-depth appreciation of the day-to-day concerns and operations of American diplomatic missions. This mutual lack of understanding tends to reinforce the episodic character of the interaction between the military and diplomatic mechanisms through which the nation seeks to coordinate and implement its foreign and military policies overseas.

NEW APPROACHES

One obvious way of changing this is to eliminate the asymmetry in the two chains of authority. This could be done by creating subregional or regional authorities in the diplomatic chain that correspond to military commands and by creating a military authority at the country level—an approach that has been suggested by a number of observers since the 1960s. The difficulty of such an approach is, however, that it could lead to a plethora of new offices and staffs in both the military and diplomatic hierarchies. The basic solution to better coordination and more effective integration of diplomacy and military operations is not to expand the bureaucracies that are involved in the effort, but to reduce and streamline them.

There are, however, some beneficial changes that could be made without going to the extremes of creating either a set of super-ambassadors with regional authority or military "country commands." The basic goal is to promote regular contact between the diplomatic and military chains of command, something that could be facilitated by expanding the authority of the regional and subregional commanders and country ambassadors to arrange military exercises, conferences, port visits, and operations with foreign nations on their own with general policy guidance from Washington. Part of the reason there is relatively little initiative along these lines today is a hangover of the old era, when we tended to see things in a global context. Because we assumed we were locked in a global contest with the Soviet Union, political-military activity in any given part of the world had to be assessed and evaluated in terms of its impact elsewhere. Accordingly, we leaned over the years toward relatively centralized management of overseas political-military interactions. One result was that initiative in seeking such interactions atrophied at the lower levels—which contributed to a growing separation between the military and diplomatic chains at the regional and country levels.

The end of the bipolar world, along with its connotations of a global military confrontation, justifies shifting the authority for initiating, planning, and implementing that interaction downward into the hands of unified commanders, their subordinate military commands, and the U.S. diplomatic missions assigned to individual countries. Given the authority to work more closely together and to initiate political-military interactions and planning, these levels in the two chains of authority would not find it difficult to arrive at a working relationship. Modern communications—teleconferencing, among others—makes this possible; the mechanisms to accomplish it already exist. It would not be difficult to establish standing liaison offices between the military regional and subregional commands and U.S. missions in selected countries or to alter and expand the role of the attachés already assigned there along these lines. As hard as it is to move away from the centralized way in which political-military interactions were conceived and planned in the past, there is little reason now not to do so.

There are new reasons why we should try. If we are to use military forces to help set the conditions for assembling multinational coalitions in time of need, then those forces will be better able to do so by moving away from the kind of periodic combined military exercises that have been characteristic of the Cold War and toward prolonged, regular combined operations. Operating, as opposed to exercising, with foreign militaries demands much closer, longer association with those militaries, and achieving it will require the U.S. commanders and diplomatic personnel on the scene to work together far more systematically and intensely than they have before. They should be given the authority, incentive, and resources to do it.

Chapter 5

Operations

As we speculated about what all the changes in the world meant for naval operations, we discovered we were on an intellectual path leading to changes that many in the Navy and Marine Corps would call revolutionary. The logic pushed in that direction, and one after another, many of the operational concepts and traditions we had spent most of our careers learning faded—to be replaced by new ones.

Given the changes in the world, and some of the implications of these changes, changes in the way we have operated our naval forces are almost inevitable. In some respects, these changes are quite significant, calling for a revolution in doctrine and training. To get a sense of why, it might be helpful to sketch the implications of the basic operational concept that dominated Navy thinking through the 1970s and 1980s.

THE PAST: NAVAL OPERATIONS HONED FOR WORLD WAR III

From the late 1960s to the early 1990s the United States sized and shaped its Navy to fight the Soviet Union. Although naval forces were usually part of the nation's responses to the myriad international crises that had very little to do with the superpower confrontation, the prospect of such a confrontation ran through how the Navy thought about its role, how it trained, and how it planned. By the mid-1980s, these activities reflected what we called "The Maritime Strategy."

Operationally, this strategy demanded large-scale naval operations, with the surface battle forces organized and armed to defeat the massive air, submarine, and surface attacks the Soviets would have launched against them. The Navy, therefore, planned and trained in terms of carrier battle groups, often combined and operating as multiple-group battle forces. These were potent assemblages of naval power built around the strike and defensive air power of carriers, defended by numerous other surface combatants, supported by other ships, and capable of sustained, independent operations in the open ocean, far from the arena in which the Army and Air Force would be fighting.

Planners tended to see the role of attack submarines and the Marines as independent and distant from what the carrier battle forces would be doing in the event of war. They increasingly assumed our attack submarines would operate on their own, far in advance of the surface battle forces. Submarines provided the primary antisubmarine capability of the fleet and, as such, were essential to the battle groups. But they also had strategic roles, both for attacking Soviet ballistic-missile submarines and, with the addition of nuclear-armed cruise missiles, for providing strategic nuclear offenses. As long as the Soviets believed American submarines were poised to attack their strategic nuclear reserve forces or were moving close enough to attack the Soviet Union with nuclear weapons, they would, the U.S. Maritime Strategy argued, keep their own submarines oriented to the defense, away from the vital sea-lanes across the Atlantic.

To make the strategy work, the Soviets had to be convinced that U.S. submarines would deploy forward, well before the carriers and their escorts could fight their way close enough to pose a threat to the Soviet mainland. To convince the Soviets of an immediate offensive threat from the attack submarines if the Warsaw Pact attacked into Western Europe, U.S. submarines had to be in position to attack immediately, before the Navy's surface battle forces, operating hundreds of miles away, had joined the battle.

The Marines were to land in Norway to help ensure the territorial integrity of a NATO ally. Rather than storming hostile shores, the Marines would move through commercial ports and airfields to prepositioned materiel and then deploy to defensive positions before the war started.

The dominant operational scheme, therefore, worked against the idea of integrated Navy-Marine battle operations in general—and against the notion of amphibious operations in particular. Indeed, once conflict began, it was assumed that the Navy's battle forces would operate hundreds of miles away. Planning also considered other uses for the Marines, including potential amphibious operations against the northern flank of the Warsaw Treaty forces that might be attacking in central Europe. But the notion of getting the Marines into Norway before the war began overshadowed all. The role of the Marines in the Pacific under the Maritime Strategy was less clear, for planning considered the use of amphibious operations against Soviet forces in the Kuriles and on Kamchatka. It also postulated using the Marines in the defense of Korea and elsewhere, however, in scenarios similar to the one used for Norway.

Powerful carrier battle groups remained the building blocks for peacetime operations, too, and we responded to crises with two questions: what did we need to handle the crisis at hand, and what would we need if the Soviet Union tried to intervene? The first might not call for the full power of a battle group—but the second usually did, and we planned and conducted our crisis response in terms of carrier battle groups.

The Navy, then, entered the new era with an operational concept focused on sea control that featured large, potent carrier battle forces and separate, independent operations by the submarine force and the Marines. Crisis response to anything short of a global war with the Soviet Union was considered a lesser case that did not require much deviation from the "Maritime Strategy."

NOW AND THE FUTURE: NAVAL OPERATIONS FOR THE NEW ERA

The strategic milieu now is quite different. The planning context is regional, not global, and no potential enemies currently have the capacity to challenge the United States for control of the world's oceans. The military technological revolution is upon us. By the fall of 1992, the Navy leadership was prepared to lay out a new operational concept.

In September 1992 the Navy promulgated a new white paper entitled ". . . From the Sea," which emerged from a profound debate about the future role of naval forces. It marked a major shift in U.S. naval doctrine and implied significant change in the size, structure, and operations of the nation's naval forces. The core of the new concept is power projection, and it envisions naval forces participating directly with the U.S. Army and Air Force to control events ashore. The focus of U.S. naval operations has shifted from an open-ocean confrontation with another military superpower to joint military operations in littoral areas, against militarily inferior opponents.

Overall, the ideas outlined in ". . . From the Sea" and in the series of subsequent statements, doctrine, programs, and operations signal as profound a change in operations as any that have emerged in the last century.

The Focus on Battlefield Support

". . . From the Sea" reorients the primary focus of U.S. naval forces from sea control to land control. Affecting events on land is not a new concern of naval forces. But in consort with the Marine Corps (or mobile Army units), the Navy's new operational concept goes far beyond the traditional notion of power projection to a broader concept, better understood as battlefield dominance.

This is not to rule out all other potential targets of naval power, nor to suggest that U.S. naval forces will no longer be concerned with the maritime capabilities of potential opponents. On the contrary, the new operational concept anticipates and recognizes a continuing operational need to strike power plants, transportation nodes, and other targets that may be great distances from where the ground forces of an opponent may be operating. It also accepts as axiomatic that local sea and air dominance are required to affect battlefield outcomes.

But the new operational concept argues that the primary purpose of U.S. naval power in conflict is now to help bring about a desired outcome on the land, directly, and that the primary military opposition the United States will face in doing this will be an opponent's ground forces.

Regional Reach

The concept of regional reach borrows from some of the arguments advanced in the U.S. Air Force's 1990 white paper, "Global Reach, Global Power." Some in the Navy believe this was a less-than-subtle assault on the proposition that the United States must maintain a strong overseas military presence. But I think the Air Force's white paper is focused on a deeper argument and recognizes that new technologies enable the United States to bring its military power to bear against potential opponents sooner, over much greater distances, and with more precise, more devastating effect than was commonly understood. This argument rings true.

I think each of the military services has entered an era in which the temporal and spatial aspects of military operations will be very different from those of the past. All the services now benefit from global surveillance and intelligence systems that offer real-time understanding of an opponent's actions. The range of each service's weapons is stretching farther and farther, too, and all these developments change the notion of concentration of force. They allow the United States, and perhaps only the United States at this time, to concentrate firepower on targets without first placing military forces relatively close to those targets. Long-range-strike systems, combined with broad-coverage surveillance and command systems and precision-guided munitions, allow all the U.S. services to step beyond the operational constraints that have existed up to now.

In the Navy's case, these factors demand that we think not in terms of tens of miles but in terms of thousands of miles. Formerly, we paid a great deal of lip service to the capacity of the fleets to influence the activities and plans of an opponent many miles away, but the new concept goes beyond forcing an adversary to consider how fast U.S. naval forces could appear just offshore. Now, overseas-deployed naval forces should normally operate as if they could directly affect events throughout a region, not in days or weeks, but in minutes and hours. The power of U.S. naval operations stems more from the way we distribute and coordinate it among widely dispersed naval components than from the capacity to concentrate those forces near where we want to focus that power.

Consider the following examples. We normally associated naval operations against regional predators with relatively short distances. We launched carrier air strikes against the enemy in North Korea from less than one hundred miles off shore. Yankee Station, the site of carrier operations during the Vietnam War, was about the same distance from the coast. In both wars, we conducted virtually all the maritime-interdiction and naval-gunfire-support missions within sight of the shoreline. We conducted naval operations against Libya, Lebanon, Iraq—and in nearly all the three hundred crises since the end of World War II—from just beyond the horizon. We positioned naval forces globally, but we brought the actual military power embodied by those forces to bear within distances measured in tens or, at most, in hundreds of miles.

More recently, however, we have operated within a broader, regional context. During Desert Storm, carrier-based aircraft conducted strikes from carriers located in the Red Sea and—one thousand miles to the east—from the Persian Gulf. In addition, we used naval forces throughout the Mediterranean in a coordinated, regional defensive operation called Med(iterranean) Net.

Med Net referred to an air surveillance and defense screen established across the length of the Mediterranean and oriented southward. The undertaking depended on land-based radars, AWACS, and strategically placed Aegis-capable surface ships. It involved land- and carrier-based aircraft and featured a command and communications structure that allowed the Sixth Fleet flagship's command center to monitor and control the air space over the entire Mediterranean. Neither the Libyans nor anyone else challenged Med Net, so we will never really know how effective a defense shield it was. We do know, however, that it provided surveillance certainty and greatly increased allied peace of mind.

Peacetime—Conflict Operations

Deterrence favors a rapid-response capability, but this does not require naval forces to deploy overseas as if on the brink of war. In the past, there was a strategic rationale for doing so. In the context of the zerosum thinking that drove operations during the Cold War, we assumed a constant state of confrontation with another superpower. As a result, the deployed forces were primed to go to war. They responded to crises in which there was no direct Soviet involvement as if the Soviets were hovering in the wings, and remained ready to control and dominate escalation if the Soviets tried to intervene.

Today there is no need for that. I am not suggesting we would ever want to deploy forces incapable of coping with the situation we expect, nor advocating low readiness on the part of the forces we deploy. Structuring and deploying forces as if war was always imminent, however, is no longer necessary.

This prompts a new operational flexibility. We can change the configuration of the forces we deploy in peacetime. Most such operations, for example, may permit us to deploy smaller forces than the carrier battle groups used traditionally and to use different mixes of force. Fairly standard carrier air wings with every aircraft carrier is no longer the only way to do it. For some presence missions, what counts is not the continual presence of a full-up carrier air wing but the carrier itself—and the implication that we can quickly fill it with whatever mix of combat aircraft a particular contingency may call for by flying the aircraft aboard when needed.

Changing Interservice Relationships

These new operational considerations—the focus on battlefield support, the notion of regional reach, and the operational flexibility in the mix of deployed naval assets—alter the operational relationship between the Navy and Marines, change surface- and submarine-force operations, and create a new operational relationship between naval forces and other U.S. military forces.

They require, for example, a deeper, different integration between the Navy and Marines. As ground forces, Marines are the only naval instrument that can directly control territory. Under the old Maritime Strategy, the Navy–Marine Corps relationship was one of strategic coordination but hardly one of strategic integration, for we expected the Navy and Marine Corps to operate separately, in different arenas, against different kinds of forces. Over the years, we expressed those expectations in operational compartments that grew further apart.

The operational concept now, however, demands integration, not just coordination, between the Navy and the Marines. The central naval problem is now one of crossing hostile littorals and imposing the military power of the United States onto the land. The seas are no longer the potential battle areas they once were. Now they are the highways, the runways, and the bridges over which the United States can bring its forces to bear against a land power. The Navy must ensure that the transport of

U.S. military power occurs rapidly, smoothly, and safely, but it will also participate directly in the land operations and, indeed, may be the first U.S. force component to do so. The Navy and Marine Corps now are wedded to a common operational effort that will take place in the same arena, against the same kind of forces, in a common contest, not for control of the high seas but for dominance of the battlefields ashore. As the naval-forces component most capable of controlling land, the Marines are central to the Navy's operational concept in ways that go far beyond that called for by the outdated Maritime Strategy.

The new operational concept calls for a different relationship between U.S. attack submarines and surface battle forces, too. Submarines will continue to provide the sea control that is necessary, but they will operate together with surface forces in new ways in the littoral. This means changes for both components, but coupled with technological improvements, revolutionary changes in submarine operations are in the offing.

A similar conceptual shift has taken place regarding the relationship between U.S. naval forces and the Army and Air Force. The notion of regional rather than global conflict means that all the military services will focus on the same general arena, in the same general location. The Navy's new operational concept recognizes this. Indeed, if there is a single goal of the concept, it is to enable the application of joint U.S. military power in littoral areas, which means integrating the power of naval forces with those of the other services.

An Operational Template

To meet the demands of deterrence in this new era, naval forces will be required to react quickly to fait accompli efforts by regional predators. This is in part a question of capabilities. It requires, for example, that naval forces be able to pose a threat to an opponent's ground forces, for those are the forces most likely to be used in fait accompli scenarios. It also implies a particular kind of operational approach. In practical terms, this means some combination of regular overseas deployments and the capacity to surge additional forces quickly in time to prevent, disrupt, or delay potential opponents' operational schemes for their ground forces. Not all the naval forces necessary to accomplish this have to be on the scene when the crisis erupts, but we must be able to conduct a very rapid buildup if the situation dictates.

Because deterrence revolves around the perceived capacity to counter a regional predator's ground, air, and missile forces, naval forces should, in theory, operate regularly in a way that supports this perception. That means day-to-day operations integrated with friendly ground and air forces—U.S. Marines, Army and Air Force units, or the ground and air force components of alliance and potential coalition partners. This, in turn, implies operations and training that build skills in providing surveillance, intelligence, and targeting information against an opponent's ground-force operations and skill in providing close air support, interdiction, and other supporting fire to friendly ground forces. These operational skills will provide the best means by which U.S. naval forces can help maintain existing alliances and build the conditions to assemble multinational coalitions in times of crisis.

Getting the right answers to the following specific questions will be central to success in the new era.

—How should the Navy and Marine Corps configure their forces and assets for the broad range of operations and crises the nation will face in the years ahead?
—What is the operational meaning of jointness?
—What does Navy–Marine Corps integration mean?
—What do all these considerations say about the operational requirements for submarines, surface ships, and naval aviation?

FORCE CONFIGURATIONS IN THE NEW ERA

Shifts in naval operational concepts are bound to drive changes in the way naval forces organize for operations. The Navy has, in fact, begun to test and exercise new force configurations and has adopted a new vocabulary to signal the changes. One of the most prominent of the new terms is "Naval Expeditionary Forces," a general rubric reflecting the growing interest in greater operational flexibility, an orientation toward tailoring forces for particular missions, and a commitment to integrating Navy and Marine Corps assets to better meet the exigencies of littoral warfare.

The choice of "expeditionary" is partly symbolic. We meant it to signal forces configured specifically to project power ashore, as opposed to defeating opposing fleets on the open ocean, to emphasize Navy–Marine Corps integration and to connote the commitment of military forces for specific military goals.

Desert Storm required the Sixth Fleet in the Mediterranean to do more with less. The carriers were in or on their way to the Persian Gulf and Red Sea, but the requirements in the Mediterranean never got smaller—in fact, they grew. As a result, we had to innovate with different force configurations; in a way, the results were a revelation. The smaller configurations had much more capability than we had earlier thought, and some of them, such as the maritime action group, turned out to be more useful in some instances than the larger, carrier-centered battle groups.

This is more than just semantics. The new lexicon of U.S. naval-force operational configurations was consciously designed to free operational thinking from the assumptions of the past and, in particular, from the idea that virtually all operations revolve around the power of the carrier battle groups so prominent in the old Maritime Strategy. These may still be the best way of organizing and using naval power in larger-scale military contingencies, and we may need the overwhelming capabilities of a carrier battle group in some deterrent efforts. Yet it is important to remember that the new terms are semantic wedges designed to shift naval operational doctrine toward a different, more flexible way of operating.

The Naval Expeditionary Task Force—NETF

A Naval Expeditionary Task Force (NETF) is the core naval force for major regional conflicts. It is designed to provide a cohesive Navy–Marine Corps team for littoral operations and to operate with Army and Air Force units—or their foreign counterparts—to provide integrated sea-air-land power projection. Circumstances may require a particular mix of ships, systems, force units, and weapons, but notionally the following ships and aircraft would make up a task force:

—1 CV/N (1 carrier wing)
—1 large-deck amphibious ship (LHA or LHD)
—2–3 smaller amphibious ships
—6–9 surface combatants (with TLAM)
—2 SSNs (with TLAM)
—logistics support
—maritime-patrol aircraft (land based)

We designed the NETF to provide four capabilities: power projection; battle-space dominance; command, control, and surveillance; and sustainability. Table 5:1 indicates actions we would expect an NETF to perform in each of the major categories.

Operations Short of Regional Conflict

While major regional contingencies may be the most demanding kinds of problems facing the United States in the next several years, they are not the most likely. History suggests that less-demanding military contingencies will be the norm. NETFs can be tailored to deal with these. An NETF can, for example, provide two Naval Expeditionary Task Groups (NETGs), one built around the aircraft carrier and one built around a *Tarawa* (LHA 1) -class or *Wasp* (LHD 1) big-deck amphibious assault ship.

Each of the task groups would include fixed-wing aircraft and helicopters, surface combatants capable of providing area air defense, sub-

TABLE 5:1 NETF Military Activities

Power Projection	Battle-Space Dominance	C3I/Surveillance	Sustainability
Close Air Support	Sea Control	C3/Forward Surveillance	Air Ops: 12 hr/day
Manned Strike	Local Air Superiority	Coordinated Intelligence Fusion	Ground Ops: 15 days
Unmanned Strike	Enforce Sanctions	Joint Force Air Control	Sea Control Ops: 30 days
Noncombatant Evacuations	Maritime Interdiction	Joint Task Force Command	
Hostage Rescue	Counter-Drug Ops		
Amphibious Raid	Air-Defense Suppression		
Special Operations			
Security and Humanitarian Assistance			
Peacekeeping/Peacemaking			

The USS *Wasp*. This versatile ship class will become the center of Naval Expeditionary Task Groups.

marines, logistics-support ships, and varying size Marine Corps ground units or special-operations forces. Although not so powerful as the total task force, each group could operate independently at considerable range from one another. Each would carry the capacity to link and operate with land-based units and to provide the command, control, and communications necessary to conduct moderate-scale joint and combined military operations.

It is worth noting that a task group with a big-deck amphibious ship is functionally similar to a task group with a larger aircraft carrier. Noting the functional similarity represents a major change from the way we saw the two ships in the past, when LHAs and LHDs were identified solely with amphibious operations. These versatile ships, which carry short-take-off/vertical-landing AV-8B Harriers and helicopters, are as large as World

War II *Essex* (CV 9) -class carriers. They are multipurpose platforms; when combined with surface combatants, submarines, and land-based air, their NETG can perform a range of missions—from sea control to power projection—formerly associated only with carrier battle groups.

In addition to providing two task groups, a task force can furnish a number of smaller Naval Expeditionary Task Units capable of a wide range of activities and operations. What the Sixth Fleet calls a maritime action group—two surface combatants and a nuclear-powered attack submarine supported by land-based maritime-patrol aircraft—is an example of a task unit. Such units can give alliance or potential coalition partners the technical edge they need to make their own forces more capable—which enhances our political influence and lays the basis for multinational coalitions in times of crisis. As a relatively small unit of U.S. naval power, such task units are ideal for the kind of local initiatives supported by regional and subregional commanders and their diplomatic counterparts.

As the notional-force packages portrayed in figure 5:1 indicate, the NETF will be able to provide U.S. unified commanders with many force

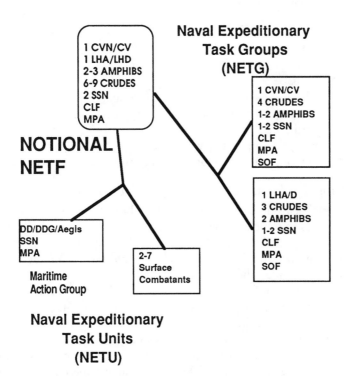

FIGURE 5:1 Notional Force Packages from a Single NETF

options and the ability to tailor forces for a wide range of simultaneous requirements short of regional conflicts.

NETF Operations in Major Regional Conflicts

The number of NETFs needed for regional conflict will depend on many variables. There are, however, some general considerations concerning regional conflict that would determine the configurations of the task forces—and that afford some insight into the number we may need.

Some overseas basing is likely to be available in any conflict the United States enters in the next decade. The United States should not, however, assume that adequate basing will be immediately available. Accordingly, a task force can sustain its operations independent of land bases, and the forces that comprise it can help obtain basing if it is not available—or expand it if what is available is not sufficient. This means that task forces must be balanced and relatively powerful in each of the four combat categories listed above. Specifically, any task force will provide the command and control facilities necessary for a joint-task-force commander to control at least the initial stages of a joint military campaign involving, for example,

—two U.S. Army divisions
—250 U.S. Air Force tactical aircraft
—three NETGs.

It must also be able to dominate the battle space and project sufficient power to maintain control of the military situation until the United States can bring its heavy land-based power to bear. Whatever number of task forces the contingency requires, they must arrive on station quickly and work together smoothly with ground-based forces.

Peacetime Deployments and Adaptive Force Packaging

The normal peacetime deployments of naval forces affect response times and the rates at which the unified commander can assemble the forces needed to cope with crises. Planning as if the United States is going to have the numbers of ships it has today would be wrong. Here again, things are changing. The total numbers of ships the United States has in its active forces is decreasing, and unless we make radical changes in the way we deploy ships overseas—and in the personnel and maintenance policies that support these deployments—the numbers overseas at any given time during peacetime will also decrease.

Yet, it would also be wrong to assume we need to deploy naval forces the way we have in the past. NETFs are divisible to permit greater flexibility in overseas deployments, not only because the numbers are declining, but also because the strategic context no longer demands the kind of continuous powerful carrier-battle-group deployments we maintained during the Cold War. The United States already has moved away from the continual carrier-battle-group and amphibious-ready-group forward deployments it once maintained, and this trend will continue.

Smaller and less powerful configurations may actually be better suited for alliance maintenance and coalition building. As the fundamental rationale for U.S. overseas military presence shifts away from providing a nuclear umbrella and toward the ideas of offering a new kind of deterrence and technological complement to the capabilities of alliance or coalition partners, the appeal of smaller, rather than larger, naval-force configurations will become more prominent—which leads to the concept of adaptive force packaging.

The term has several connotations. It assumes fewer forces will be available to provide overseas presence, but it also assumes that the purpose of forward presence is changing and that different force configurations can serve effectively. Adaptive force packaging combines and tailors forces from each military service for scheduled overseas deployments and backs them up with units that remain in or near the United States. The idea differs from traditional forward deployments in several respects.

First, it requires all the units earmarked for possible employment overseas to train together to meet the most likely contingencies and operations in a given region. The intention is to facilitate much closer joint training and operational awareness by the various Army, Air Force, and Navy components designated as a particular joint deployment package. Second, during peacetime deployments, only a portion of the entire joint-force package—tailored to meet the contingencies the overseas commander believes most likely to emerge—actually deploys. The units that deploy act as the advance elements of the entire joint-force packages, the remainder of which are available for surge deployment if needed. The approach stimulates much greater experimentation, innovation, and flexibility in the way we configure the forward elements of the entire force package.

Overall, Naval Expeditionary Forces and adaptive-force-packaging concepts evolved from a different way of thinking about conflict operations and overseas presence in the new era. In the past, the Navy tended to think almost exclusively about how many carrier battle groups—each capable of self-sustaining, independent military operations—were needed for these purposes. They were our unit of measure. Now, and increasingly in the future, we will plan more flexibly, in terms of assembling a force tailored more precisely for the particular problem at hand, using different units of measure depending on the mission.

The unit of measure for overseas presence, for example, is likely to be a Naval Expeditionary Task Unit, while the unit of measure for combat operations will normally consist of an entire task force. With respect to crisis response or the problem of deterring regional predators, a single task group can function as the advance element of the full task force, a concept that fits neatly with the notion of adaptive force packaging for crisis management.

JOINT MILITARY OPERATIONS—LIVING JOINTNESS

Joint operations are taken as a given in formal Department of Defense pronouncements, and it is almost impossible to find someone who professes to be against these. The unanimity with which we endorse them, however, is not backed up by an in-depth, well-articulated understanding of what joint operations are or how they are to be conducted. There is, to be sure, some agreement. By definition, joint operations involve more than a single service component, and most military professionals would argue that the fundamental reason for having joint operations is to increase overall combat effectiveness.

It had been an experiment, really, a joint exercise that featured an Army major general controlling the ground forces involved in the exercise, an Air Force major general controlling the Air Force and Navy air assets, and a rear admiral controlling the naval forces. Nothing new there. What was new was that they all did it from the carrier Saratoga. *When the two-week exercise ended, the consensus among the flag officers involved was clear and strong: the key to effective military operations in the future was to "live jointness" every day.*

Competing Views of Jointness

Beyond these common understandings, however, the consensus breaks down, and there are at least two competing notions about how to use different force components to increase combat effectiveness.

One view argues in favor of using the best qualified force component for a given mission—that is, to enhance combat effectiveness by fitting forces to the missions for which they are specialized—this is the specialization argument. The other seeks to achieve higher combat output by combining or integrating forces. This is the synergism argument. These definitions do not really represent two sides of the same jointness coin, however. Accepting one or the other will ultimately lead to very different operational behavior and force structures.

Several years ago, someone asked Gen. Colin Powell, Chairman of the Joint Chiefs of Staff, what he meant by joint operations. "Consider all the forces available to a joint

Army Special Operations MH-47s onboard the *George Washington*. Joint operations and adaptive force packages will become a way of life in the years ahead.

commander as if they were provided as the contents of a tool box," he said. "The commander would pull from the box the forces he needed to do the job, regardless of whether the tools were painted Army, Navy, Marine Corps, or Air Force. That's what joint operations are."

An advocate of specialization would say that the former Chairman of the Joint Chiefs was exactly right. The advocate would go on to explain that the joint commander would turn to the toolbox and pick the right tool for the job. If the job required a strategic-bombardment campaign, the commander would assign that mission exclusively to the force component that knew the most about strategic-bombardment campaigns— perhaps the Air Force component commander. If the contingency also required maritime interdiction, that assignment would go exclusively to naval forces. The commander would continue carefully fitting the various missions to the force specialized to conduct them.

An advocate of synergism also would say that the former Chairman was exactly right, hastening to explain, however, that the joint commander should turn to the toolbox and build the right tool from the various force components. If the job required a strategic-bombardment campaign, the joint commander would combine the air assets available from all the components in the most productive way, assembling capabilities with little regard for the uniform worn by the men and women charged with particular missions.

The difference is subtle but significant, and the operational implications vary greatly. The essence of the specialization view is to differentiate combat responsibilities clearly along service-specialty lines. The essence of the synergistic view is almost the opposite, at least regarding mission assignments. Specialization advocates argue that their approach takes advantage of the inherent efficiency of the integrated traditions, doctrines, discipline, and procedures of a single service. Synergists argue that blending the particular strengths of each service on a mission basis provides higher combat output than any single service could produce on its own. These views lead down separate paths to different practical understandings of joint operations.

The specialization view, for example, ultimately favors a command-and-control system that focuses on keeping the responsibilities and operations of the various service components distinct and separate. The interaction among the service components, in this view, should concentrate on maintaining the distinctions and keeping the lines of responsibility from overlapping because mission exclusivity would keep the components from getting in one another's way and allow each to carry out its particular specialty with greatest effectiveness. There is synergism in this approach, for if each service component meets the demands of its particular mission, the result will be an effective, smoothly conducted war or operation. If the Air Force, Navy, and Army components focus, respectively, on the air campaign, the sea campaign, and the ground campaign, the overall operation will benefit. The Air Force's resources will not be diluted by allocating sorties to support Army ground operations; the Navy's resources will not be "stretched" between providing naval fire support to the ground campaign and destroying the opponent's naval forces; the Army's resources will not be "diverted" to protecting Navy or Air Force bases.

Is this an exaggerated extension of the inherent logic of this view? Yes, but it is essentially the logic that girds the spirited defense each military service makes in justifying its own aircraft, specialized communications, and logistics systems.

The logical extension of the synergism view generates similar problems of unreasonableness. Pushed to its extreme, it not only dismisses the idea that there is benefit to maintaining separate service traditions, doctrines, and procedures, it ends up arguing in favor of full military unification and of differentiating among forces strictly in terms of functional capabilities. Moving too far in that direction would probably undercut the ability to recruit, train, and prepare the men and women who will make up the force.

I have exaggerated these two views to highlight their differences. In the real world, of course, the contrasts are not so dramatic, and as Desert Storm demonstrated, the use of force in any real conflict is likely to involve aspects of both. It is important to note, however, that these two potentially very divergent ideas lie beneath much of the discussion of joint operations. Neither has yet been proclaimed as the prevailing concept; both have legitimate claims on becoming the dominant view—which leads to two suggestions.

The Practical Meaning of Jointness

The first is to promote the kind of day-to-day activities by the services that will arrive at a practical balance of the two views. Largely because of Adm. William Crowe's and Gen. Colin Powell's active interest in developing an in-depth understanding of joint operations during their tours as Chairman of the Joint Chiefs of Staff, the military has come a long way. On average, there are more joint exercises each year than at any time since the end of World War II.

It's hard to argue, however, that there will ever be too many. More important, we in the military must go further in trying to work out the practical meaning of jointness and in defining where the right balance really lies between the contending views. I think we have to move beyond the idea of joint exercises toward the goal of operating jointly on a continual basis. This notion is a challenge both to the current joint command structure and to the peacetime activities of all the military services.

It challenges the existing joint command structure and current pattern of activity because it argues for creating standing joint commands (as opposed to joint task forces) at the tactical level, the level of command most often engaged in actual combat—at the corps, fleet, and numbered air force levels in the Army, Navy, and Air Force, respectively. Joint commands currently do not extend down to this level, and while joint-task-force commands do, these are almost always formed for specific operations. To facilitate the day-to-day interactions necessary if we are to give practical meaning to jointness, then, we should organize standing joint-force commands, at the three-star level, which would maintain direct operational command over the units of the four services that would otherwise operate together for particular missions or crises. The continuing character of a standing joint command would help make "jointness" real. The practical, pragmatic meaning of jointness will emerge as the operational forces work out all the myriad aspects of what joint operations should entail.

We in the military do not, however, have the luxury of putting off thinking about what joint operations should be until the details are worked out. The Navy in particular should define what we think joint operations imply because we have committed ourselves to them both in the way we expect to use naval forces and in the designing, structuring, and sizing of the naval forces of the future. Documents such as ". . . From the Sea" formally state that the primary role of naval forces is to "enable joint operations in littoral areas," and we have told Congress and the American people that we will build a Navy better able to do this.

With regard to the earlier distinction I made about the two underlying definitions of jointness: I think the Navy ought to line up behind the notion of synergism. It is more compatible with the idea of enabling; it helps link our rhetoric to reality better.

Enabling Joint Military Operations

"Enabling" has a temporal character. It connotes the ability of forward-deployed U.S. naval forces to be the first on the scene of a crisis, and if they cannot contain the crisis alone, to secure the beachheads and prepare the way for the arrival of U.S. ground forces and land-based air power. Once this is done, naval forces are to fight alongside those forces and, after the goals of the operation have been achieved and the other U.S. forces have withdrawn, to cover the post-conflict period.

There is more to it. The notion of enabling should extend throughout these stages, and naval forces should operate continually with the purpose of aiding and facilitating the operations of the other service components involved in conflict. The Navy should operate naturally in such a way that we help the Army do what it must do and assist the Air Force in doing what it must do. This does not posit a subordinate or a unique role for naval forces; the Army and the Air Force should add this notion of enabling to their operations. It does not mean the Navy can or should abandon its classical conflict focus on control of the seas, even if the seas we are most likely to focus on are in the littorals of the world. It does mean that we must look at the priorities of conflict and peacetime operations from the perspective of the other services and act accordingly. Here are some illustrations.

Enabling the Buildup of Ground Power

The U.S. Army, recognizing the changes in the world and, in particular, the likelihood of fighting where it does not already have forces, has been developing its own understanding of expeditionary warfare.[1] This is not the place to discuss the concept that is emerging in detail, but one of its key aspects is the need for a sequential, rapid buildup of Army power. Briefly, the Army's answer to the problem of fielding a combined arms force rapidly in a potentially hostile environment focuses on deploying units in a logical sequence; those arriving early must be capable of defending themselves, preparing for the arrival of larger, heavier units and protecting their arrival. Thus, the Army normally plans for the early deployment of units that can provide air and ballistic-missile defenses.

The sequential approach to the buildup of power has long been a central tenet of the Army's view of expeditionary warfare, and the Army has long recognized the inherent tension between building its strength sequentially, in a defensible manner, and building it rapidly. It takes time for the early units to get in place, and the rate at which following units can arrive and take their places is a function of the lift and reception capabilities that will be available. There will seldom be enough airlift to deliver everything everyone wants to get to the theater of operations early, and the early airlift of ground-based air and ballistic-missile defensive systems would eat up airlift precisely when competing demands are highest.

The Navy's role in assisting the buildup of Army power has traditionally been to deliver Army weapons and materiel to the intended debarkation points by sea lift. There are other ways the Navy can cooperate with the Army, however, to increase the rate at which the Army can build its strength abroad. One is by providing or assisting in establishing the air-defense and ballistic-missile-defense screens that are a key early step in the Army's buildup sequence. Another is to attack enemy land forces through focused surveillance, intelligence, and weapons fire from tactical aircraft, naval guns, and sea-based missiles, including the Tomahawk land-attack missiles and seaborne versions of the Army's tactical missile systems (ATACMS).

Because of their mobility, sea-based systems can provide air and ballistic-missile defense of any coastal area. Operationally, this means they can extend a defensive umbrella over the area, enabling systems such as the Army's Patriot or Theater High-Altitude Air Defense (THAAD) to move ashore.

Sea-based defense would be of particular use in a regional conflict that placed a premium on the rapid buildup of U.S. land forces. Moving land-based batteries into position eats up airlift. A sea-based system is just what a regional commander would want as the first step in a deployment, and it could also ease the competition for airlift considerably by providing the defensive umbrella to allow later introduction of a land-based system—or it could obviate the need to deploy a land-based system at all.

Cooperative Engagement and Forward Passes

A more synergistic approach would deploy a land-based system's fire-control radars and link them with missiles deployed offshore. The largest airlift requirements in a land-based ballistic-missile-defense system stem primarily from the missile and missile-support components. Transporting only the radars initially would ease the demands on airlift early in the deployment—when the competition for it would be high.

The cuing and communications used for either sea- or land-based defensive systems is technically capable of supporting this "forward-pass" concept. The land-based acquisition and fire-control radars, located at the extremities of the coverage provided from the sea-based defense system, could identify a "basket" into which ships could launch missile interceptors. The land-based components would then assume control of those missiles and direct them against incoming ballistic missiles. This cooperative arrangement would extend the range at which the sea-based missile-launching platform could destroy ballistic missiles, and it would ease the early demands on airlift, thus allowing a more rapid introduction of other shore-based ground and air units.

Enabling Strategic Bombardment Campaigns

Strategic bombardment evolved from the search for a way to avoid the heavy casualties of ground-force attrition warfare. In its modern form, it is a compelling expression of the idea of decisive force. Near-simultaneous, relatively quick, and sustained destruction of the linkages that connect the opponent's leadership to its forces, the argument goes, can paralyze an opponent's operations. Precision-guided munitions, coupled with rapid, comprehensive, systematic, and accurate target acquisition and battle-damage assessment, make this possible.[2] An air campaign that melds this argument with advanced military technology is an example of decisive force, as opposed to overwhelming force, because it attains war goals quickly without annihilating the opponent's military forces.

The theory's validity is a contentious subject, largely because many see it as an argument for shifting defense resources to the Air Force. I think this concern is unwarranted. It is important, however, to note three basic points about strategic-bombardment campaigns:

—Whether they are called strategic-bombardment campaigns or not, we should maintain the option of bringing U.S. military force to bear in the manner strategic-bombing theory describes.
—The issue facing the nation's naval forces is not whether strategic-bombardment theory is absolutely correct; it is how best to contribute to successful strategic-bombardment campaigns.
—The answer to this question will revolve around how all U.S. military services can operate together in conducting such campaigns. Successful strategic-bombing campaigns will be the product of joint U.S. military operations. They will not be the purview of a single military service.

He was the first U.S. Air Force liaison officer to join the Sixth Fleet while we were at sea, and he had one of the worst bouts of seasickness we had ever seen. It was a subject of some mirth in the wardroom; some wags suggested it confirmed everything they had suspected about how poorly organized the Air Force was for missions the Navy considered routine. But the attitude changed. The colonel recovered, and as the days went by he told us about the Air Force—what it did and why it did it the way it did. It was a revelation. In retrospect, the experiment was a profound success. He changed the tone of wardroom discussions, and he did something much more important—he helped build a new tenor for Sixth Fleet operations.

That said, what does it mean, in practical terms, to say the nation's naval forces should enable a strategic-bombing campaign, and in particular, what should their relationship be with the U.S. Air Force during the process? Part of the answer lies in what are the keys to a successful strategic-bombing campaign. Two of the most important are accurate, timely intelligence about the opponents' operational schemes and the key command and control nodes and links through which they hope to implement those schemes; and the judicious, efficient use of all the military assets that can attack those potential targets.

Accurate, timely, and complete intelligence is the key to a successful strategic-bombard-ment campaign, for if we strike the wrong targets and miss the critical nodes, then the tremendous potential military leverage of precision-guided munitions is nullified. As an Air Force manual puts it, "Air power is tar-geting, and targeting is intelligence."

Many of the targets that become key to strategic bombing are discernible long before opponents make a move. They are embedded in the physical infrastructure of their nations, and many of them—the roads, bridges, communications towers relied upon to wage war—are truly fixed targets. Effec-tive targeting, however, depends on know-ing which of these potential targets are the important ones and where the critical nodes for the opponents' operations will be when those operations begin. That is a more difficult task. Acquiring this intelligence depends absolutely on surveillance and the products it generates before hostilities begin, and on the capacity, once hostili-ties have started, to keep track of both our efforts to destroy these vital nodes and the opponents' efforts to overcome or circumvent our bombardment.

No single service can do this alone. The problem is far too complex. It can be done jointly, however, by all the U.S. force components work-ing together to collect, process, analyze, and disseminate the necessary information. The contribution of naval forces to this process will be essential, for they are the forces most likely to be on the scene before the strategic-bombing campaign begins. Tied into the nets through which other sources of information flow, they can provide the on-scene intelligence and assessment so key to effective targeting. Submarines can gather information covertly; surface vessels and aircraft—manned and unmanned—and special-operations forces inserted clandestinely can gather the entire spectrum of signals intelligence.

The efficient use of attack assets is another necessary component of a successful strategic-bombardment campaign, and efficiency stems in part from good targeting—picking the key targets and destroying them when their elimination will have its greatest effect. It also involves getting the needed destructive output from each of the attack assets committed to the campaign—which is a function of close coordination with supporting and participating forces.

Stealthy aircraft, such as Air Force B-2 bombers or F-117 attack aircraft, are deadly and efficient attack assets. We can use them in areas where an opponent has heavy antiaircraft defenses, and because they are highly survivable aircraft, we can employ them and their pilots repeatedly. Armed with precision-guided munitions, they are capable of destroying virtually any target in a single sortie. They are more effective when they operate in concert with diversionary attacks by other aircraft—which naval forces can provide—with air defenses suppressed—which naval attack and electronic-warfare aircraft and cruise missiles can do—and when updated, real-time target information is made available—which naval manned and unmanned aircraft can provide.

The efficient use of attack assets also means that vagaries of weather and the reduced effectiveness of the B-2 and F-117 during daylight should not limit strategic-bombing campaigns. The success of a strategic-bombing campaign depends on severing many links in an opponent's command-and-control system more or less simultaneously and on keeping them severed for an extended period. This simply cannot be done by attacking only at night, and given that the leverage of stealth is greatest at night, it means that other aircraft must conduct the campaign during the day. Against heavily defended targets the most effective weapon in daylight is likely to be the sea-based Tomahawk land-attack missile or the extended-range, standoff land-attack missiles (SLAMs) launched by Navy or Marine Corps F/A-18s.

Finally, the efficient use of attack assets in some cases may preclude their use for air defense. In the aftermath of the Gulf War against Iraq, there was considerable debate over the extent to which naval aviation contributed to the success of the strategic-bombardment campaign. I believe a great deal of the discussion was a bit narrow-minded because it focused on how many precision-guided munitions Air Force and Navy

Two B-2 stealth bombers rendezvous with a KC-135 tanker over Edwards Air Force Base. The Navy will increasingly be called on to increase the potency of assets like the B-2 in joint campaigns. (U.S. Air Force)

aircraft used, respectively—bean-counting, by anyone's definition—and missed the bigger picture.

One of the reasons Air Force tactical fighters were so effective in bombing missions, for example, was because the Navy controlled the air space over the Persian Gulf. Had this not been true, the Air Force would have been required to do it and to do so would have had to divert some of its most effective strike aircraft to air-defense missions. Such synergism often gets overlooked. It is, however, one of the prime examples of how naval aircraft enabled Air Force aircraft to make their contributions to the success of the air campaign in Desert Storm.

The key to successful strategic-bombardment campaigns is the effective use of precision-guided munitions. This depends in the first instance on coordinated, focused surveillance and intelligence. We can best achieve this by blending the assets of all the military services with the special perspective of national space-based assets. It means practical, operational links between Air Force assets such as Rivet Joint RC-135s that provide electronic surveillance and reconnaissance with the Navy's

EP-3s and ES-3s. Together, these assets can provide a better electronic map of an opponent's forces than either can do separately. It means tying together the tactical assets of the two services, also; working together, Air Force and Navy manned and unmanned vehicles can provide a far more comprehensive picture of the campaign than either can do working alone. It means strategic-air-campaign coordinated planning that flows naturally because the planners have done it before in war games, seminars, and day-to-day operations until it has become second nature.

NAVY–MARINE CORPS INTEGRATION

The Navy and Marine Corps were sister sea services. We all knew that. But we also knew that this sibling relationship had not always been harmonious. As we worked out the operational implications of the new operational concept, we wondered just how far this notion of integration would be acceptable. It was going to be so comprehensive that cultural traditions—such as the ideas that ground-force commanders should not have Navy ships and submarines under their command, or that Navy and Marine Corps fixed-wing aircraft should be segregated—were going to be opened up, too.

The term "naval services" connotes integrated, closely coordinated planning and operations of the U.S. Navy and U.S. Marine Corps. It is a key aspect of the Navy's new operational concept, laid out in its white paper ". . . From the Sea." This document presents it not as something that already exists, however, but as something to be achieved.

The Navy and Marine Corps have worked together since their beginnings, and the interdependency of the two military services is rooted in the nation's origin. Their traditions and combat experiences are intertwined. Their budgets are component parts of the Department of the Navy budget. Few other organizations have been as integrated as the Navy and Marine Corps. As the continuing debates over what happened at Guadalcanal half a century ago attest, few institutional relationships have been subjected to as much discussion, assessment, and rhetoric as the relationship between the Navy and Marine Corps.

In some respects, however, these two military services are less integrated than outsiders might think. As suggested earlier, the Navy–Marine Corps relationship under the old Maritime Strategy was one of strategic coordination. Each relied on the other to meet the dictates of the strategy, the Marines depending on the Navy for transport, the Navy depending on the Marines to help control essential land areas.

Yet this was not integration: The Navy focused on sea control and the destruction of Soviet maritime power; the Marines trained to defend allied territory. The Navy focused on defeating Soviet sea and air forces; the Marines focused on defeating the armored and motorized regiments it expected to face in Norway or Asia. Each service analyzed, planned, and budgeted accordingly.

As time passed, the services expressed those expectations in operational compartments that grew further apart. To the Marine Corps, fixed-wing aircraft were properly land-based, devoted primarily to close air support; integrating them into carrier air wings would simply draw them away from where they were needed. To the Navy, fixed-wing Navy aircraft were properly carrier-based; placing them ashore would keep them from the battles at sea. Navy aviation had relatively little need for training in close-air-support missions; Marine Corps air had relatively little need for training in intercept operations far at sea.

Both naval services tended to see the shore as a sharp dividing line not only for command and control but for combat specialization—with the Navy oriented toward war at sea and the Marines focused on land battle. This division was reflected in the way the two services viewed logistics. If they were going to operate separately, perhaps hundreds of miles apart, were not separate logistics structures required? These kinds of divisions were pervasive; they penetrated into training, doctrine, staffing, and operational command and control. Sometimes they led to questionable duplication.

The trend toward greater separation increasingly raised questions about the efficacy of the operation that, since the early 1930s, had been the intellectual foundation for Navy–Marine Corps integration: amphibious assault. Navy planners increasingly considered amphibious operations as anachronistic diversions of resources and attention. Even the Marine Corps found itself struggling to sustain and articulate the strategic rationale for amphibious operations.

The Significance of Conceptual Change

That the central purpose of naval operations is now to affect events on land has shifted the operational relationship between the Navy and the Marine Corps—and, for that matter, between the Navy and the Army as well. If the old Maritime Strategy in effect made the Marines naval infantry—whose strategic purpose essentially was to facilitate the fleet's operations on the high seas—the new concept reverses the Navy–Marine Corps roles, in effect making the Marines the spearhead of naval operations and the fleet a primary means of facilitating Marine Corps operations ashore. This goes far beyond the Navy's traditional responsibility of lift and naval gunfire support for amphibious operations. Indeed, pushed to extremes, the new operational concept argues that Navy operations should be integrated into Marine—or Army, or allied—operations ashore, particularly if you believe that ground forces are the final arbiter of events ashore.

This extreme view is, of course, unlikely to prevail in operational planning. It is too radical a departure from the assumptions that have driven naval thinking since Mahan, and there are honest differing views about how military forces can affect events on land. It is clear, however, that the new naval concept of operations growing from the Navy white paper ". . . From the Sea" moves the Navy toward support of (indeed, integration with) Marine Corps operations ashore.

Operational reorientation is not solely a Navy phenomenon. The Marine Corps's operational relationship to the Navy must change under the new concept also, particularly concerning what the Marines now define as their primary focus: "operational maneuver from the sea." This concept calls for moving combat power from the sea to shore in areas where opponents are weakest, and fighting maneuver-warfare campaigns aimed at destroying important nodes in the enemies' defenses, and—maneuver warfare again—rolling up the opponents' defenses by avoiding their strengths and exploiting their sensitivities and vulnerabilities. Maneuver from the sea places a premium on broad-area surveillance, intelligence, and rapid movement across relatively great distances.

It will be possible only if the Navy and Marine Corps operate as a team. Neither movement from the sea to the shore nor combat on land will be as effective as envisioned by the new doctrine unless the Marines fully exploit the surveillance, intelligence, target acquisition, and C3I capabilities of the naval expeditionary forces offshore. Exploiting opponents' weaknesses and avoiding their strengths demands real-time, precision intelligence, much of which will be generated or transmitted by the ships, aircraft, and communications capabilities brought by the Navy. Deceiving the enemy and blinding enemy sensors are important to the Marines' operational scheme, and many of the assets the Marines need to help them do this are based aboard Navy ships.

In contrast with the assumptions of the old Maritime Strategy, the Navy and the Marines are now expected to engage the same kind of enemy forces, in the same area, at the same time. As a result, the dividing lines between training, doctrine development, staffing, and operational command and control—and the duplications they generated—are no longer applicable. The rationale for the lines we drew between the naval services earlier no longer exists.

What "Integration" Means

What does integration mean, practically, and how should it be achieved? Ultimately it means eliminating some of the mental, behavioral, and financial lines we drew between the operations of the Marine Corps and the Navy. Some remain useful—perhaps essential—to command and control, and they maintain the distinct traditions that are important to morale. Many of them, however, must be erased.

This is under way. The Naval Doctrine Command, established early in 1993, will bring formal doctrinal statements and the processes used by the Navy and Marine Corps to develop operational doctrine into closer alignment. We will consolidate aviation training, and there are a number of experiments under way that will ultimately meld staff functions. All of these have important implications, and all are examples of how some of the old divisions are eroding. Some issues, however, are going to remain controversial. The need to move toward greater aviation integration; integrated command, control, and communications; integrated air and ballistic-missile defenses; adaptive force packaging—each of these will demand thought and discussion.

Integrating Aviation Assets

The Navy is moving to improve its ground-attack capability—of which much more later—but an improved land-attack capability in the future does not equate automatically to closer Navy–Marine Corps integration. It provides a better capacity for doing what integration requires because it emphasizes support of U.S. ground operations. A better ground-attack capability, however, must be coupled with a better understanding of and a focus on supporting ground operations before it constitutes integration. This is where other actions come in—most important, using Marine Corps F/A-18 squadrons as integral parts of carrier air wings.

Putting Marine Corps aircraft on carrier decks is hardly new, and cynics see the current integration of Marine Corps fixed-wing fighter-attack squadrons into carrier air wings as simply a way to ensure that the Navy has enough airplanes to fill the twelve-carrier force it is moving toward in the 1990s. The real significance of the move, however, is rooted in a more basic interest in reorienting naval aviation toward interdiction and close air support. Integrating Marine Corps squadrons into the carrier air wings is an important lever in this shift. These squadrons bring a profound understanding of battlefield interdiction and close air support. Bringing that perspective on board the carrier cannot help but infuse it throughout the carrier air wings. The move goes further: it helps cement the notion that carrier air wings are a flexible air asset, equally capable of operating from airfields ashore.

Current carrier-maintenance capabilities cannot operate ashore easily, and the Marine Corps does not have the capacity to support both Marine Corps and additional Navy tactical aircraft. The Navy is, therefore, developing a new approach to aircraft support that emphasizes both carrier and land-based air operations, an effort that pulls Navy–Marine Corps integration into the broader category of Navy–Marine Corps logistics integration. The integration of Marine squadrons into carrier air wings is part of a multifaceted movement toward across-the-board air capabilities.

These changes parallel other aviation developments, such as the planned modifications to the Marine Corps's AV-8B STOVL aircraft— improved night and all-weather systems plus precision-guided weapons capabilities. The improvements will make the AV-8B more comparable to the fixed-wing attack aircraft that normally operate from carriers. This, in turn, begins to erode the distinction between the carriers and the amphibious assault ships normally associated solely with amphibious operations.

The Navy has embarked on a course that will blur the functional distinctions we once made between the ships that carry aircraft and the kind of aircraft they carry. We are moving toward full Navy–Marine Corps aviation integration, not only because we will call on the carriers and their Navy aircraft to provide the kind of aviation support to U.S. ground forces that traditionally has come from the LHAs and LHDs, but also because we may use these same LHAs and LHDs to perform such missions as sea control—that traditionally have been the province of the big carriers. The LHAs and LHDs are versatile platforms, with impressive communications capabilities that will improve dramatically in the years ahead. Exercise data are increasingly showing that they can be used not only in their traditional amphibious roles but in a much broader range of tasks.

During her initial deployment to the Mediterranean in November 1991, for example, the USS *Wasp* (LHD 1), a modern 41,000-ton amphibious assault ship with sixteen AV-8B Harriers embarked, teamed with the Sixth Fleet Maritime Action Group to form a sea-control task group. We designed the exercise specifically to see how this kind of task group could deal with the surface, subsurface, and air threats typical of regional conflicts. As such, it focused on using the Harriers in antisurface and counter-air roles, in addition to their ground-attack missions. The exercise was successful, confirming the flexible capability inherent in naval forces. The concept has its limits, including a lack of organic airborne-early-warning capability, which we anticipated. Range and armament limitations constrained the Harrier's effectiveness, and using this kind of Navy-Marine task force in a U.S.-Soviet war would be risky. Fortunately, those risks do not exist today. Against the threat posed by regional-conflict scenarios, LHAs and LHDs are clearly sea-control platforms.

Integrating C3I

Future warfare will place major emphasis on communications systems, computers, and C3I architecture. The Navy and Marine Corps must improve their ability to mesh their capabilities. Planned upgrades will permit naval forces, afloat or ashore, to make better use of surveillance systems like JSTARS and AWACS. This is one of the keys to giving the carriers a dramatic increase in their ability to support forces ashore. The communications upgrades will give aircraft carriers and the LHA/LHD big-deck amphibious ships a capability to host joint-task-force commands, regardless of the uniform worn by the joint-task-force commander. The capacity of the communications channels that link forces at sea with forces ashore will expand greatly, offering the real-time, all-source, and precise intelligence needed if the Marines are to exploit fully the concept of maneuver warfare. Those same channels, backed by the full global capabilities of the United States, will provide broad electronic bridges for forces operating throughout the region, affording them the degree of situational awareness required to dominate regional opponents.

In a broad sense, then, improving C3I capabilities can eliminate the artificial line at the beach that we have assumed separates Navy and Marine Corps responsibilities. Integrated C3I builds a different model of operations, moving away from the notion of specialized and separate spheres of operational concern and toward the vision of a single operational sphere. The logical extension of this, of course, challenges the tradition that a naval officer commands the operations of ships offshore, while a Marine Corps officer commands units ashore. There is no compelling reason why naval forces charged with supporting a campaign ashore should not be under a common commander—Navy or Marine.

Integrated Air/Ballistic-Missile Defenses

Planned C3I capabilities will also create a new theater-ballistic-missile defense potential. Just as the planned sea-based theater-ballistic-missile defenses allow the Aegis-capable sea platforms to work synergistically with the Army's land-based THAAD or Patriot PAC-3 systems—largely because of the improvements in naval C3I—so, too, are they able to work with radar associated with the Marines' improved-Hawk air-defense systems. Linking Aegis capabilities with the air-defense acquisition and fire-control capabilities of Marine radars could extend a sea-based ballistic-missile-defense umbrella much farther inland, setting up the forward-pass arrangement sketched previously. New C3I capabilities will be necessary, but they are coming; using them could further weld the Navy and Marine Corps into a single operational team.

Marines in Adaptive Force Packages

Growing operational experience also points to new definitions of what Navy–Marine Corps teams can do. We have used carriers to conduct noncombatant-evacuation operations (NEO), but this has normally taken place in concert with amphibious ships carrying Marines. In the future, the United States may not have the time to assemble such forces because such missions can occur with very little warning. Now, however, we may not need two different kinds of platforms.

Operation Safe Haven, conducted late in 1991, tested whether a carrier could support both the force insertion and evacuation requirements, as well as the combat air patrol and strike needs of a major NEO undertaken in a hostile environment. Accordingly, the USS *Forrestal* (CV 59) embarked four hundred Marines and ten helicopters. The carrier was then able to generate both the strike and combat-air-patrol missions—routine for a carrier—as well as the assault and extraction-force missions normally launched from amphibious assault ships. The concept worked, and additional tests of Navy–Marine Corps integration are now a central part of the U.S. Atlantic Command's concept of adaptive force packaging. Innovative ways of combining the potent capabilities of the sea services are proving out. They are the wave of the future.

The full meaning of Navy–Marine Corps integration will emerge as we experiment, exercise, and face real-world operations together. That is as it should be, for the world remains too unpredictable to define the complete meaning of integration by edict. But the trend is clear and correct: integration is coming.

SUBMARINE OPERATIONS

U.S. nuclear-powered attack submarines are the ultimate blue-water sea-control asset—a position they achieved in the wake of World War II when two nearly simultaneous changes occurred. One—nuclear propulsion—was technological; the other—a focus on antisubmarine warfare—was operational.

Nuclear propulsion transformed World War II's fleet boats from submersibles, which actually spent most of their operating time on the surface, to true submarines—ships whose normal operating environment lies beneath the surface. And as Soviet submarine capabilities grew, the focus of U.S. attack-submarine operations dwelt increasingly on antisubmarine warfare.

By the mid-1960s the meaning of sea control had grown from the capacity to dominate the oceans' surfaces and the air above them to the ability to control the undersea realm, for it was in this realm, more than any other maritime arena, where the ultimate correlation of naval power between the United States and Soviet Union was defined. U.S. submarine superiority stemmed in part from technology—our submarines were quieter and had better sonars. It also stemmed from the training and experience of the American crews, for they honed their skills in very real—but largely unreported—missions against adversaries operating on the front line in the Cold War.

U.S. submarines have never been fully isolated from what transpires on land. Indeed, the strategic role of the nuclear-powered ballistic-missile submarines (SSBNs) dealt almost exclusively with targets on land—and many of today's nuclear-powered attack submarines (SSNs) can conduct long-range cruise-missile strikes against land targets or deliver special-operations forces ashore.

Yet we should not underestimate what the shift to joint littoral warfare means to U.S. undersea operations and doctrine. We optimized the U.S. attack-submarine force for containing Soviet maritime power, and the new operational concept for U.S. naval forces challenges many of the ways our submarines operate day to day. In the past, Navy SSNs trained primarily to detect, trail, and destroy Soviet nuclear-powered submarines. While they sometimes operated in littoral areas, we designed them for deep-water, open-ocean operations. While they sometimes operated near U.S. surface forces in coordinated operations, they more often operated independently, often far from other U.S. forces. While they occasionally transmitted data to other U.S. forces, they were much more likely to operate in a receive-only mode. While they provided intelligence, surveillance, and strike capabilities, they did not focus on an opponent's ground forces, and we assumed there was no role for U.S. submarines in ground battles.

The fundamental operational question now facing the U.S. submarine community is therefore how to apply the submarine's basic strengths—stealth and endurance—within the context of the new operational focus on joint military operations in littoral areas. Based on my experience, I believe that they can make the necessary operational changes expeditiously and that the answers that emerge will not reduce their capacity to refocus on deep-water ASW, should that become necessary in the future.

The New Submarine Role: Battlefield Support

How can our submarines contribute more directly to the success of U.S. operations on and above the land? One way is to provide covert surveillance throughout those operations. Surveillance missions, of course, are not new to U.S. submarines, but surveillance operations in the future will be different. The target of submarine surveillance efforts will shift toward a potential opponent's ground-force activities and intentions.

Pending ground-force operations are often heralded by naval and air force activities, and U.S. attack submarines have provided information on such activities in the past. Beginning now, we need to supplement and complement submarine surveillance activities focused on such indirect indicators with information that deals more directly with ground-force deployments and capabilities.

Most military tacticians would accept that covertly monitoring what opponents do with their ground forces before hostilities begin has a high payoff if conflict ensues. Preconflict training, exercises, and force dispositions all provide indications of an opponent's capabilities—and, more important, intentions—and if we can observe them undetected they can be relatively accurate guides. Submarines cannot see everything. They must remain submerged offshore to remain covert, and traditionally, the reach of a submarine's electromagnetic and optical sensors has been a function of the limited height attainable by the boat's mast and antennas.

New technologies, however, can extend the submarine's surveillance reach. Underwater autonomous vehicles and unmanned air vehicles, for example, both controlled by the submarine, are two ways of extending the submarine's surveillance vista, and using the submarine as a long-term covert base for special-forces operations can provide direct linkage with on-the-ground surveillance of an opponent's ground-force activities.

This will alter the traditional submariner's view of communications, however, for it is likely to require the submarine to transmit to a much greater extent. A thousandfold increase in the amount of data that the submarine will be able to receive will be here by the end of the decade, and new communications modes will enable submarines to transmit and relay data without being located. As the revolution in data collection, sorting, and dissemination continues, submarines can become full partners in the flow of tactical intelligence. The capacity of submarines to become even greater surveillance assets is expanding, not contracting.

Submarines can help ground forces in other ways. In the kind of missions foreseen for special-operations forces, it may be important to put as many as 100 to 150 special-operations personnel ashore as a single unit from a submarine. Equipped with high-technology communications, a unit this size could direct fire sufficient to disrupt, immobilize, or even destroy very large enemy forces. In acting as a long-term base of special-forces operations, submarines may have to remain in relatively shallow water, on or near the bottom, for extended periods. While this mode of operation is not common today, there is no reason why our submarines could not operate in shallow water—in seventy to eighty feet of water compared with the two hundred– to three hundred–foot minimums of the past—and in the future could rest on the bottom for as long as is necessary.

Submarines may increasingly contribute to larger-scale amphibious operations also, for covert surveillance of an opponent's mine operations can locate mine fields long before we have to cross them. In the future it would not be surprising to rely on submarines to neutralize mine fields. Indeed, submarine-controlled unmanned underwater vehicles can already provide mine detection and plotting, and the same technology shows promise for mine clearing and destruction. Submarines are probably our best weapons against the source of most mine fields—the minelayers themselves.

U.S. submarines can also play a direct strike role in disrupting or defeating an opponent's ground operations. The submarine's vertical-launch tubes, for example, could prove valuable for battlefield fire support. Armed with a range of standoff weapons—from the Tomahawk land-attack missiles to a version or derivative of the U.S. Army's Tactical Missile System (ATACMS), possibly with a new high-technology front end with "brilliant" antiarmor munitions—and tied into a real-time targeting system, submarines could play a critical role in the early stages of the nation's response to short-warning regional attacks, not only capable of attacking fixed, preselected transportation and communications nodes, but also able to engage mobile targets. A submarine with the capability of launching approximately one hundred improved Tomahawk land-attack missiles or ATACMS with antiarmor warheads could contribute significantly to strikes against either fixed targets or more mobile armed forces.

This kind of stealthy strike may appear little different from that promised by B-2 bombers, but the difference is that while it might take hours for the B-2 to deliver its ordnance after the decision to attack, it would take an on-station submarine only minutes to do so. This quick-response capability, coupled with the endurance to remain on station for extended periods before and after such an attack, could make a significant difference in the deterrence and war-fighting equations.

Antisubmarine Warfare in the Littoral

Littoral warfare implies that we must directly confront and neutralize the diesel-electric submarine threat. We cannot avoid the littoral just because an opponent's submarines may be present. Yet the littoral environment rules out some of the ASW techniques and tactics we have employed successfully in the open ocean.

We cannot rely on a sweep that is merely adequate to ensure safe passage for a high-speed transit, and we may not be able to use surface vessels and aircraft for ASW missions because our opponent may control the sea and air close to shore. The noisy, complex near-shore environment makes it very difficult to detect, track, and destroy other sub-

The USS *City of Corpus Christi* (SSN 705), is typical of the U.S. submarine power that helped win the Cold War. Now, such vessels will increasingly focus on support to forces on the battlefield. (General Dynamics, Electric Boat Division)

marines. The acoustic chaos will tend to cancel the acoustic advantage of our submarines—the sensors, weapons, and techniques that work so well in the open ocean are not necessarily effective in shallow areas close to shore.

Despite these hazards, U.S. attack submarines will remain a central and potent component in U.S. antisubmarine warfare in the shallow water of the littoral. Submarine-emplaced mines at harbor mouths can bottle up the threat. If a diesel-electric submarine has to transit open ocean to get on station, the acoustic odds will climb dramatically in our favor. The same underwater unmanned vehicles used for mine counter-measures undoubtedly have utility in littoral ASW, and continued advances in passive and active sonar will heighten our submarines' acoustic advantage. The nuclear submarine will dominate antisubmarine warfare in shallow water, just as it has in the open ocean.

Continuing Traditional Roles: Sea Control and Deterrence

Hard-earned submarine operational capabilities must not be allowed to atrophy. The submarine force must continue to provide the kind of sea control necessary to assure unimpeded access to the world's littorals, and our SSBNs will remain the foundation of strategic nuclear deterrence. Operationally, this means the task facing the submarine community is not simply one of reorienting to the new focus on littoral warfare; submariners must add such skills while maintaining proficiency in traditional open-ocean missions.

SURFACE FORCE OPERATIONS

We must ask our surface forces many questions. Are we armed with the right weapons? Do we have the right command and communications links to support battlefield operations and integration, and indeed, in the future, do we even have the right ships to perform the new missions facing U.S. surface combatants and amphibious ships? The new operational focus poses significant challenges to business as usual. Consider, for example, the operational shift in the traditional defensive mission of surface combatants brought about by the prospect of carrying out this mission almost within sight of land.

Piercing the Littoral Fog and Close-in Defenses

In the past, the defensive roles of surface combatants revolved around the problem of protecting the fleet, merchant ships, and strategic sea lift in the open ocean. The context of open ocean was important too; the assumption that we would have vast areas within which to organize the defenses of the fleet, for example, led us to think in terms of layered defenses in depth. We were able to think in terms of initial engagement areas far enough away from the fleet to destroy the platforms carrying the missiles or torpedoes with which the attacker sought to cripple the fleet.

This was a particularly cost-effective defensive mode: if we could destroy the opponent's weapons carriers prior to launch, we would in effect negate all the weapons they carried. Surface combatants fitted into this general defense scheme by contributing directly to the outer defenses, by providing the communications links between the outer ring of defenses and rings closer in to the center of the fleet, and by providing the defensive screens against those enemy aircraft, missiles, surface vessels, or submarines that might leak through the outer defensive rings. The open-ocean environment allowed relatively easy detection and discrimination of enemy aircraft and vessels, largely because the electromagnetic and underwater acoustic environments were relatively—repeat, relatively—stable and simple. Detection and discrimination are never really easy.

The defensive context of joint littoral combat, however, differs in some important respects. The basic problem facing surface combatants is no longer to defend the fleet on the high seas. It is to help impose the fleet's power onto the land by projecting power ashore. The focus is no longer on defending against aircraft, ships, and submarines traveling across vast stretches of open ocean. Now it is on the problems of removing or avoiding mine fields, neutralizing submarines in relatively shallow water, extending a ballistic-missile- and air-defense umbrella over land, and defending against stealthy, sea-skimming missiles launched directly from sites ashore.

Solutions to some of these problems are almost here. We paid for our neglect of mine warfare in the Korean War and again during Operations Desert Shield–Desert Storm; this time we have finally learned our lesson. The Navy has increased its investments in mine detection and mine sweeping and is developing new capabilities, such as air-cushion vehicles that can provide remote-control minesweeping and autonomous or fiber-optically tethered underwater vehicles for mine detection and clearing. Different operating procedures with our submarines are likely, and surface combatants will deal increasingly with positioning mine-clearing assets where we need them, assisting them in their detection and clearing tasks, and protecting them while they do this—often in high-threat areas near land.

To meet these and other challenges, surface combatants will have to extend their ability to sense and engage threats across the relatively complex, unstable electromagnetic environment typical of the land-sea interface. Terrain features will mask incoming missiles and aircraft threats longer—reducing the time available to react; radar screens will be cluttered with sea and land returns; higher densities of friendly and neutral ships and aircraft will make it harder to sort out the returns on the scope and will put a premium on identification-friend-or-foe systems; acoustic complexities will challenge sonar systems and operators; shore-based gun and missile batteries will move up on the threat chart.

While these challenges may not negate the layered defenses in depth and the other tactical concepts we perfected over the last three decades, they will, however, force us to adapt, raising the need for new technology and tactics to offset the new challenges.

Battlefield Dominance

The new operational emphasis on battlefield dominance increases the importance of extending surface-combatant power from the sea across the shoreline. Naval surface combatants and amphibious ships have a long history of providing fire and logistics support to troops ashore, and their contributions in the future will continue to involve these traditional means of support. The new operational concept, however, goes further than what for decades surface officers have considered an additional—and sometimes peripheral—concern.

Now, battlefield dominance has emerged as a prime purpose of naval combat operations. This means that a new perspective—that of the ground forces—must be inculcated in our surface forces and added to their tactics and doctrine. Surface combatants must increasingly see conflict from the perspective of ground-force combat priorities and threats. To the extent we are successful in introducing this perspective to surface-force operations, the way surface combatants contribute to command, control, and communications; surveillance; air and ballistic-missile defense; and fire support will change.

Surface combatants will be required to link sea-based and land-based capabilities by acting as integrating nodes in the theater-wide communications nets that will tie all forces together. In terms of surveillance, we will expect surface combatants to contribute directly to the theater commander's understanding and awareness of where the opponent's forces—especially land forces—are and what they are doing. Ground-force movements will become a central concern of our surface combatants.

In terms of air and missile defenses, surface combatants will become central parts of shields that extend over land and sea. While Aegis ships may provide the initial shield, allowing ground-based defenses to be established on hostile shores, they are likely to have continuing responsibilities with regard to the defense of forces ashore throughout crises or conflicts. The Med Net experience alluded to earlier is a harbinger of things to come. It will be common practice to build and maintain theater air and missile defenses by linking Aegis-capable ships with airborne warning and control systems, land- and sea-based interceptor aircraft, and land-based surface-to-air missile systems to defend both land- and sea-based forces. This will certainly be the case if the threat of low-observable aircraft and missiles increases as we think it will; integrated sea- and land-based defensive shields provide far better defenses against such threats than either could acting independently.

Fire Support

If any surface-combatant operation is affected directly by the new focus on ground combat, it is that of fire support, and this is where the view from the foxhole will have its most direct effect. The Navy's focus on joint littoral warfare leads inevitably to the notion that fire support from the sea—until recently the poor stepchild of surface-combatant operations—will become a central tactical goal.

The basic approach to fire support is not likely to change: ground units will call for fire and then direct its employment. Technology will, however, adjust this basic relationship in at least two respects. First, the designation of targets will become more precise, and second, the geographic area for fire support will expand, largely because of improved surveillance provided by JSTARS and unmanned aerial vehicles. Naval fire support will be an integral part of a joint battle space in which we will integrate, coordinate, and direct assets from all the military services within a comprehensive C3I system.

Surface combatants will be required to provide fire support throughout the theater in support of ground units as small as Marine infantry squads and as large as Army corps. They must be able to meet this demand with a range of weapons: advanced guns (probably electro-thermo chemically advanced) mounted on ships and sea-based helicopters; laser-guided weapons such as Hellfire missiles carried by LAMPS and other sea-based aircraft; missiles armed with multiple, intelligent antiarmor submunitions (like the Army's ATACMS); and Tomahawk land-attack missiles.

Greater Independence—Different Interdependencies

All of these considerations point to an underlying trend in naval surface operations that will become more visible in the next few years. It is a trend that calls, on the one hand, for greater independence in the operations of surface combatants, and on the other for new kinds of interdependencies. Clearly, the thrust of the force configurations discussed above is toward greater operational reliance on units other than what we know today as carrier battle groups.

Today's surface combatants do not spend all their time at sea in company with or in proximity to aircraft carriers, even when assigned to carrier battle groups. This operational separation almost certainly will increase. In major crises or conflict, of course, surface combatants will operate in conjunction with the carriers; but for most operations they will not. Overall, then, they will move toward greater operational independence vis-à-vis the carriers.

Joint operations will push the surface force toward new and different interdependencies. Surface combatants, operating either as maritime action groups or as larger force configurations in conflicts, will do so in much closer coordination and, perhaps, much more constant direct communications with amphibious ships and submarines than has been the case in the past. Much closer coordination with shore-based air power is coming.

Today, U.S. Army helicopter operations from the decks of our surface combatants are experiments. We view the linking of surface combatants with AWACS and Air Force fighters as a special event, and we talk about integrating surface fire support with ground campaigns as an exception to "normal" surface-force operations. Tomorrow, we will see them all—and other "operational anomalies"—as standard operating policy.

NAVAL AVIATION OPERATIONS

Naval aviation will retain its responsibility for strike, battlefield support, and air-to-air operations, but the relative emphases on these missions and the manner in which they are executed are likely to change. Battlefield support will reorient naval aviation's focus on air-to-air operations away from the open ocean to near- and overland environments. We will increasingly employ precision, standoff weapons and operate within a joint, integrated context.

We should expect to launch long-range strikes against strategic targets in conjunction with Air Force aircraft and Tomahawk land-attack missiles. This may entail operating directly with Air Force or other aircraft in attacking the same target, perhaps providing air-defense suppression for other attacking aircraft. Whatever role falls to naval aviation in an integrated air campaign, however, it will require communications and command processes necessary to mesh smoothly with other air assets under the terms of air tasking orders and other methods of coordination used to manage and direct such campaigns.

In air-to-air operations, naval aviation must have weapons that are effective over land and in the electromagnetic environment of the air-land-sea interface. Much-improved combat-identification capabilities will be necessary.

In battlefield-support operations, the requirements will be twofold: close communications and coordination with ground units, and the right kind of weapons. The former means both having the kind of communications links that allow the most effective use of aircraft in close-air- and battlefield-support missions, and a new sophistication in our overall knowledge and understanding of ground operations. The latter means an increased capacity to deliver standoff, sensor-fused munitions. Again, the ability to distinguish friends from foes will be crucial.

Generally, flexibility will be the key to successful naval air operations. This flexibility should extend to the way we associate aircraft with the ships they fly from. In the past, we associated particular mixes of aircraft with the carriers and tended to plan in terms of air wings that were assigned to a carrier, trained with the carrier as it prepared to deploy overseas, and stayed with it for the duration of the deployment. Although air wings varied from deployment to deployment and from carrier to carrier, the air wings were more-or-less standard. This air wing standardization was helpful. It facilitated personnel planning and maintenance scheduling. Each air wing had a balanced mix of aircraft that gave the carrier the capacity to provide air defense, strike, antisurface strike and surveillance, and antisubmarine warfare. The standard wing fit into the relatively static, if dangerous, bipolar world that allowed the carrier to fight in a worldwide war with the U.S.S.R. and to deal with the range of contingencies far short of that challenge.

To meet the challenges ahead, however, carriers will be more generalized aviation platforms that do not always operate with a standard air wing on board, but whose decks can be filled within twenty-four to forty-eight hours by aircraft that fly aboard when needed—in the particular mix tailored for the problem at hand. U.S. Air Force aerial refuelers make this a viable approach.

We may be able to change the numbers of aircraft we require and the relationship of active to reserve aviation units. The idea of deployed carriers with less than a full, standardized air wing aboard—coupled with their ability to mass aircraft in times of need—could allow us to operate with fewer active aircraft overall—and fewer of what are now nominal active air wings. If, for example, all deployed carriers do not have to carry a full complement of aircraft at all times, we will not need as many aircraft to support the level of overseas presence the carrier deployments provide. Aircraft not deployed could train with the Marines at Twentynine Palms, with the Army at the National Training Center, or with Air Force wings practicing coordinated strategic bombing. It could permit us to think of reserve aircraft and pilots not as attrition fillers, as is now the case, but as integral fighting elements that could fill the decks of carriers as combat units when needed.

There are other elements of flexibility that naval aviation must develop. Adding twenty to thirty aircrews to any given deck could increase the daily attack-aircraft sortie rates by 20 percent. Operations from expeditionary airfields, when feasible, could generate higher sortie rates and improved battlefield support. Many other innovations will emerge as we realize the true flexibility of the carriers—U.S. sovereign airfields operating in optimal positions to project power.

FORCE IMPLICATIONS

The chapters that follow discuss the character of future naval forces in some detail. But before we talk about future force structure and other points, it is helpful to keep several more general points in mind.

Expanded C3I Capabilities

One of the most obvious is, of course, that we will need forces that are better able to interact with one another and with ground-based forces. This is ultimately dependent on the kind of communications capabilities we build into the force, and while the Navy has done much in this regard, much more remains to be accomplished. The shift toward joint operations in littoral areas posits a very complex, densely occupied, integrated operating environment in which successful operations will depend on real-time, comprehensive understanding of what enemy forces, friendly forces, and a myriad of other intermingled participants are doing. It will require a level of communications and an overall C3I sophistication exceeding anything available today. Unless our ships and aircraft can communicate better with one another and with the other services' assets, many of the operational roles sketched above will simply be unattainable.

This means communications in the fullest sense—an understanding of what our comrades-in-arms are trying to do coupled with a technical capacity to pass vast amounts of information back and forth very quickly. This will require changing operational mores, and it will also mean technical upgrades and electronic changes. Submarines will be required to receive and send data faster and in greater volume than ever before, and submariners, who are proud to be members of the "silent service," will be required to rethink their view of communications. Surface combatants and naval aircraft will need the right kind of links to ground forces and land-based air forces, for the promise of better fire support and effective, integrated air defenses will remain unfulfilled without them.

All will need better means of separating friends from foes—our weapons have become so accurate and so deadly that we may soon dare not loose them without a better capacity to confirm the target's identity. We will be unable to meet the challenge of operations on and over the battlefield unless we solve this problem.

New Ship and Aircraft Designs

Given the roles sketched for surface forces, you have to ask if we have the right kind of surface combatants. Arguably, many more vertical-launch tubes would be useful, as would much more helicopter deck space. We may want to incorporate the V-22 tilt rotor into the kind of offensive and defensive operations outlined above for sea-based helicopters, and if so, we will need deck spaces that can accommodate this aircraft. We should think about surface ships as mother ships that carry not only helicopters, V-22s, and unmanned aerial vehicles, but also other surface craft, such as patrol craft or multipurpose air-cushion craft, and unmanned underwater vehicles as well.

The missions discussed also imply design changes. We will always need better aircraft: ones that fly longer, have lower signatures, carry more ordnance, and are more reliable. But the emphasis on littoral warfare and close-in support, among other things, will continue to kindle interest in short-takeoff/vertical-landing (STOVL) aircraft, capable of operating not only from the large carriers but from platforms like LHAs and LHDs. We may need even more capable aircraft operating from carriers much larger than today's *Nimitz* class. We will have to build a new Navy.

Chapter 6

Building a New Navy

It was Rear Adm. Riley Mixson who referred to us as the "band of brothers" after one of the many marathon sessions we had as we worked out the new vision and consensus. He said we reminded him of Admiral Lord Nelson's officers as they prepared the fleet. But I thought of the band of brothers the way Shakespeare's Henry V used the term before the great battle of Agincourt—to express the notion that they were all in the enterprise together, and that all of them, regardless of rank or station, would define the destiny of their kingdom together. That was what we were trying to do, I thought. And as long as the band of brothers worked together, we could set the destiny of the Navy.

There are obvious links between operations and forces. The Navy, perhaps more than the other military services, has always tried to make sure that the men and women who are charged with figuring out how large naval forces should be and what they should be able to do—"sizing and shaping" in the jargon we use—understand real-world operations and succeed reasonably well at their task. Those who have the most say about the size and shape of future naval forces generally, by virtue of their years of service and rank, have the most operational experience, and the Navy has developed planning processes that require the men and women who design the forces to stay in touch with those who will operate them.

Thus, one might expect that the recent dramatic changes in the international environment would be translated fairly rapidly and smoothly into the force-planning processes. That is not always so. While military organizations can cope with the major changes that began with the collapse of the Berlin wall, there are some strong reasons why the translation of political-military revolutions is neither automatically nor easily reflected in the size and shape of military forces.

Military organizations normally approach changes in doctrine, structure, and procedure cautiously. That is their nature. All bureaucracies, of course, cultivate predictable behavior and value standard, routine, and repeated patterns of decision. Within military bureaucracies, moreover, there are some particularly strong incentives for this kind of behavior. Lives depend on military personnel doing what their plans say they should do, on being where other members of the military expect them to be, and doing what they are expected to do when it is to be done. Such behavior, in turn, requires discipline, knowledge of what is wanted, and skills in execution—characteristics that are best achieved by repetition and iteration, rather than by turmoil and innovation.

The natural inclination of military organizations to avoid change normally works out well—except in periods where changes are clearly needed because the context in which the organizations operate is profoundly different. For as much as routine and iteration are necessary for good military operations and for building reliable military forces, routine and iteration that are not consistent with the political-military environment can lead to chaos. When the environment changes as much as it has over the past several years, then the bias against change becomes dangerous and must be circumvented or altered.

It is easy to make broad generalizations about change and innovation in a military bureaucracy, as if it were some kind of mechanical artifact in which you get change and innovation simply by ordering it, or by plugging in or removing parts. The Navy bureaucracy, however, is a human institution, composed of men and women who take what they do very seriously. They do what they are told as well or better than any other human institution. But simply ordering them to change, to innovate, or to build different forces, and then waiting for things to happen, is wrong on two counts. It assumes that those who issue the orders know with precision what changes are necessary (and which ones are to be avoided), and it ignores the insights, intelligence, and vast wisdom that reside inherently within the bureaucracy. The right sort of change and innovation in building future forces comes from energizing, tapping into, and channeling that pool of wisdom.

This entails removing or loosening organizational barriers that inhibit the flow of insights and perceptions, altering decision-making roles, and adjusting the rules governing how the decision-makers interact— something the Department of the Navy tried to do between the summer of 1992 and the summer of 1993. Along with a number of others, I participated in this attempt, and it is worth talking about what we saw. It may have something important to say about how to initiate change in any large institution or bureaucracy. It also says something about how the Navy is building future naval forces and what those forces will be.

AN INSIDER'S PERSPECTIVE: 1992–1993

From the perspective of naval officers in the Pentagon and in the fleets early in 1992, the world had been transformed. The Soviet Union had dissolved. Desert Storm had been a national military triumph, but the Navy left that conflict with deep questions about the efficacy of its operational doctrine in the post–Cold War era—and reservations about the weapons it had developed under that doctrine. The presidential campaign was reaching stride, and the prospect of a major shift in the government was growing. Major budget reductions were in the wind. A consensus was growing within the Navy leadership that the Navy had to change—perhaps radically—to cope with what was a truly new era.

That was the essence of the times. But this description captures neither the mood nor some of the underlying currents that merged in the summer of 1992. It was a period of intellectual turmoil and concern and of fragmenting consensus among senior naval officers, a fragmenting that stemmed from the West's victory in the Cold War. That four-decade conflict had, after all, defined the professional concern of the naval officers assigned the task of sizing and shaping the nation's naval forces for the new era. It had given meaning to everything we had done in our chosen profession. While we relished the victory as much as any American, we were professionally much more interested in and concerned with the inevitable postwar question of "Now what?"

We were concerned because the Cold War had given us an underlying consensus on what was to be done. It provided a basic rationale for reconciling deeply held differences of opinion over how billions of dollars were to be spent each year, about how we should size and shape our forces, about what our planning priorities should be, and about how to blend the warfare specialties that each of us had served, learned, and believed in. Now the consensus, along with the Cold War, was gone.

The disquiet this generated was more pronounced within the Navy than in any of the other services. Both the Army and the Air Force had come home from the first of the new-era conflicts—Desert Storm—with their entering doctrines intact. The AirLand Battle concept that the Army developed after Vietnam held up well in Desert Storm's one hundred–hour ground campaign, and the concept of strategic bombardment, long an Air Force doctrinal belief, seemed vindicated by the victory. Naval personnel served with distinction and courage in the Gulf War. There was no question of that. But while the Army and Air Force came out of the conflict believing that the operational concepts they had developed during the latter decades of the Cold War were still valid for the new era, this was more difficult for the Navy to do. The Army and Air Force had a doctrinal cushion upon entering the new era that helped maintain their internal professional consensus. The Navy did not.

There were other signals that things were wrong. Major naval aviation programs, for example, had faltered or been canceled in a manner suggesting that the Navy did not know what it wanted to do in the future, or if it did, could not efficiently manage the programs necessary to get it there. By the summer of 1992 the explosive issues of sexual harassment and the role of women in the Navy had surfaced in what was soon to be called the Tailhook scandal. The scandal was doubly traumatic for the Navy, for it not only raised the particularly difficult and sensitive issue of sexual harassment, it also suggested that the professionalism of the officer corps had eroded.

There were concerns, usually unspoken, about who was going to define the Navy's destiny in the new era. Two years earlier, in 1990, there had been a pervasive sense of optimism within the flag ranks of the Navy. By all objective measures, the 1990 Navy was the best since World War II. The investments of the late 1970s and early 1980s were manifest in modern equipment and weapons. Morale, readiness, and the quality of naval personnel were dramatically higher than they had been a decade earlier.

The implications of the end of the old era had not yet been thought about as much as they would be, and few, if any, questioned whether the Navy that had been built over the previous two decades could adapt to a new era. Instead, there was a general sense that the prospective budget reductions and force drawdowns—which virtually every flag officer knew were coming—would be absorbed mainly by the Army and Air Force. From the 1990 perspective inside the Navy this seemed obvious. The collapse of the Berlin Wall, the pending conventional-arms-control agreements covering U.S. forces in central Europe—all of this spelled a shift of U.S. Army and Air Force units back to the United States from their forward deployments and a growing reliance on the Navy as the nation's first line of defense. Thus, while the overall defense budget was clearly going down, the Navy's share of it would decline more slowly, and perhaps not at all. That was the 1990 view.

Yet, the base force proposed initially by Gen. Colin Powell, Chairman of the Joint Chiefs of Staff, and adopted as the Defense Department's plan in 1991, undercut that prediction. It reduced the size and the budgets of each of the military services. The reductions were not particularly dramatic, certainly not by subsequent standards, and they were spread roughly evenly across all three military services. But, the basic approach taken by those who drew up the base force did not conform with what Navy flag officers thought would occur; they had missed their guess. The base force seemed to have been defined by the Chairman of the Joint Chiefs of Staff. He obviously had the authority to do this, but to many it suggested a diminution in the Navy's say over what its destiny was to be.

These undercurrents had merged by the summer of 1992, dampening the optimism that had prevailed two years earlier, and building a growing sense that something had to be done. Secretary of the Navy William Garrett resigned in July under the shadow of the Tailhook scandal. He was replaced by Sean O'Keefe, then serving as Comptroller in the Secretary of Defense's office, who saw the need to signal a dramatic change in Navy thinking. Drafts of the Navy's white paper sketching the new operational concept were circulating within the Navy staff and in the fleets. Internal Navy assessments, comparing the thrust of the white paper drafts with the Navy's fiscal year 1994 program—then being prepared according to the dictates of the base force—indicated significant discrepancies between what the Navy would formally pronounce as its operational concept and the way it would propose to allocate resources when the program went to Congress in the fall. The climate seemed almost supersaturated with the potential for changes.

What we needed was a new consensus on what the new Navy should be. The basic problem that summer was an absence of consensus and, in its absence, a growing sense that the Navy had lost control of its destiny. If we could forge a new consensus, this anomie would end. How were we to achieve it?

Defining the problem as a need for a new consensus within the Navy in large part reflected the general management orientation of the Chief of Naval Operations, Adm. Frank Kelso II. Before his appointment to the senior Navy position, he had developed an appreciation for the management philosophies of J. Edwards Deming, the organizational theorist often credited with the dramatic success of Japanese manufacturing productivity in the 1970s and 1980s. Deming's views—known as total quality management, and adopted as "total quality leadership" (TQL) by Admiral Kelso—held that the productivity of any human organization was tied to a shared commitment by its members to explicit, relatively specific goals. The view was hardly revolutionary, but Deming also argued that a true collective commitment to specific organizational goals was unattainable without a free flow of discussion among the members. He offered a number of techniques and procedures that could facilitate such interplay, even in highly hierarchical organizations like the military. Admiral Kelso was convinced the Navy could and should adopt the Deming approach before he became CNO, and he introduced it shortly after his appointment.

As concerns over a lack of consensus on the future size and structure of the Navy grew in 1992, the search for a means of applying the TQL approach to building such a consensus intensified, paralleled by a growing sense on the part of senior Navy leaders that the traditional Navy staff organization could not contribute to a solution and, in fact, worked against it. By midyear Admiral Kelso had reached the same conclusion. A major staff reorganization was announced in August and implemented by the following October. It was a change unprecedented since World War II.

STAFF REORGANIZATION

Although the Navy staff had been reorganized from time to time since the 1970s, its basic structure had remained intact. For roughly two decades, decisions within the Navy about the allocation of resources had been worked out by a staff structure dominated by three major spokesmen: the vice admirals who advocated the perspectives and resource claims of three Navy communities. These were the so-called "staff barons," a term meant to imply their relative independence and equal power status. Their fiefdoms were naval aviation, surface warfare, and submarines, plus the research, development, and acquisition bureaucracies that worked for and within these platform categories.

This is not to argue, of course, that other offices on the Navy staff were unimportant. Concerning decisions on the size and structure of the Navy, however, the "platform sponsors"—the barons—had the greatest influence. Each had direct access to the Chief of Naval Operations. Their prominence in Navy force-structure decisions and the vocabularies used in their deliberations had been part of the overall effort during the 1970s and 1980s that emphasized designing, programming, and budgeting for a sea-control Navy.

By the late 1980s, resource allocation within the Navy did, in fact, reflect the dominance of sea control. The Navy staff understood the warfare areas and used the argot associated with them, but the perspectives of each of the platform sponsors had not been amalgamated. The pattern of budgetary decisions, for example, continued to show a remarkable stability. Every Navy budget submitted to the Secretary of Defense from the early 1970s on was divided similarly, with each platform sponsor ending up with about the same portion as it had in previous budgets. The tradeoffs across platform sponsors that had been anticipated never seemed to occur, and when made, they were imposed by the Secretary of Defense, or Congress—never the Navy.

In retrospect, it is difficult to criticize what happened, for the overall results were a conformity between the Navy's operational concept of sea control and the acquisition process—and it is not difficult to understand how this came about. For the most part, the barons' influence tended to be solidified rather than diluted. Each had the same formal rank within the staff, and each had the same authority to appeal to the CNO any decision that did not result in budgetary balance among the platforms.

As the years went by, the result was twofold. On the one hand, each of the platform perspectives took on the orientation and vocabulary demanded by an overall emphasis on sea control. The strategy was, after all, institutionalized within the resource-allocation and acquisition processes that determined the character of the Navy. On the other hand, this institutionalization took place within the trifurcated structure of decision influence that stemmed from the power of the barons, which inevitably made them the foremost defenders and advocates of the sea-control strategy.

That said, no one can deny their magnificent performance. They built, equipped, and trained the Navy that is at sea today, the most effective Navy in the world and one of the principal contributors to the demise of the Soviet Union. In retrospect, the staff organization built in the 1970s fit the times. The problem in 1992 was that times had changed.

The Demise of the Barons

The reorganization announced in the summer of 1992 did several things:

—It formally charged a staff office, designated N-83, with representing the views of the fleet commanders in chief in the requirements and resources process; and it created another office (N-85), headed by a Marine Corps major general, to forge a closer link with the Marine Corps.

—It downgraded the platform sponsors' rank to that of rear admiral and—removing their direct access to the Chief of Naval Operations—made them subordinate to the office now charged with ranking and consolidating each of their claims on resource allocation: the Deputy Chief of Naval Operations for Resources, Warfare Requirements, and Assessment (N8), a vice admiral.

The reorganization was driven by several factors. Congress had directed the military services to reduce their numbers of flag and general officers and was generally supportive of any reorganizations that did so. As the presidential campaign accelerated during the summer, the Bush administration welcomed any symbol that it managed foreign and national-security military policy making decisively. By the summer of 1992, moreover, the Joint Staff had emerged as a new and important player in the task of defining force-structure requirements—a factor that argued for aligning the Navy staff structure more closely to the functional concerns of the Joint Staff.

Yet beneath the bureaucratic concerns lay a more fundamental motive.

The reorganization was also driven by the awareness that if the Navy was to go beyond the rhetoric of change and actually incorporate the tenets of its new operational concept into the size and structure of naval forces, the influence of those institutions within the staff that had become the bastions of the older Maritime Strategy had to be altered. Downgrading the rank of those charged with managing and representing the views of particular warfare communities was not sufficient to do this, for they would retain their authority and would be required by their bureaucratic positions to represent parochial views. Having them report directly to one of the CNO's subordinates, rather than directly to the chief, was no guarantee either that the allocation of resources among them would be made on the basis of the new operational concept, nor that the representatives of the various communities would subordinate their views as community spokesmen to some collective sense of what was best for the nation. Staff reorganization was a necessary step to change this.

The reorganization greatly bolstered the institutional power of the Deputy Chief of Staff for Resources, Warfare Requirements, and Assessments (N8). In addition to subordinating the barons, some decision functions previously divided among several staff offices were consolidated in the new N8 office. Earlier, for example, the function of assessing the extent to which each of the baron's resource desires fit with an overall scheme and the function of actually allocating resources in the form of the Navy program and budget requests had been divided among separate offices: the reorganization consolidated both of these functions into the N8 office.

As the title indicates, the Deputy Chief of Naval Operations for Resources, Warfare Requirements, and Assessment (N8) that emerged from the staff reorganization had the staff authority to establish requirements for future naval forces, allocate money among those requirements, and judge the implications and effectiveness of the allocations. The office is, of course, a staff office. The recommendations made by the vice admiral holding the job have effect only if approved by the Chief of Naval Operations, the Secretary of the Navy, and the Secretary of Defense. Only with their approval can the recommendations get into the President's budget request to Congress. Few staff offices in any of the military services, however, have the kind of potential bureaucratic power the Navy staff reorganization gave to N8.

THE JOINT MISSION AREAS ASSESSMENT PROCESS

Organizational modification may have been necessary for the new strategy to become more than rhetoric, but it was not sufficient. It was necessary to incorporate new standards, or criteria, for deciding program priorities, a new vocabulary to the debates over how to allocate the budget, and a new style of decision making. These were required, in part, to break up the old categories and compartments consistent with the earlier strategy, and in part to develop quickly a new corporate sense of direction within the Navy. Both structure and process had to change if the shifts in strategy called for by ". . . From the Sea" were to be implemented by the new Navy.

The Navy had used several processes over the years in attempting to reconcile the different perspectives of the warfare communities and to allocate resources among the various advocates. By 1992 the process that held sway was referred to as the Navy Program Appraisals and, before the staff reorganization, was the responsibility of a Deputy Chief of Naval Operations for Naval Warfare, OP-07 in the nomenclature of the time. This deputy was separate from the deputy charged with formulating the five-year Navy program, but the appraisal process he headed was designed in theory to provide a collective staff view of priorities in the Navy's areas of strike warfare, antisubmarine warfare, antiair warfare, and antisurface warfare—a view that relied on detailed analyses of the military effectiveness of the programs advocated by other staff offices, and especially on the program preferences of the platform barons.

Over the years, however, the appraisal process had become complex and routinized and by 1992 was increasingly viewed as a bureaucratic drill. It seemed to be driven by a rigid schedule and a plethora of reiterated analyses that slipped ever deeper into esoteric detail. This, in turn, made the appraisal process more the preserve of the lower-ranking staff members and their contractor supporters than a process in which the flag leadership could interact on substantive discussions. They became instead simply authenticators of whatever their staffs pounded out, and the changes in the Navy program coming from the appraisal process became incremental and certainly less noticeable as one appraisal replaced another each year.

The architects of the new assessment process wanted to change this. They sought to immerse the flag officers in an ambitious effort to develop a broad new understanding of the future size and structure of the Navy and the Marine Corps. They expected to deal with the possibilities of sweeping changes rather than adjustments, and they realized they had to draw on the collective wisdom of the most experienced members of the naval service, which dictated that the flag and general officers play a much more direct role in the process.

The heart of the new process involved a new program assessment structure. That structure (see figure 6:1) was essentially a matrix that made program advocates justify their programs in terms of their contri-

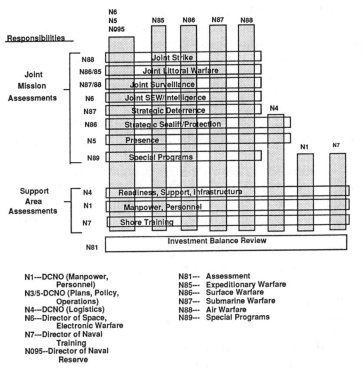

FIGURE 6:1 The Joint Mission Area Assessment

bution to the new mission areas. Discussions within each mission area ranked the programs that applied to that mission area, and a process called the Investment Balance Review determined the overall ranking of all the programs. The final rankings represented a consensus within the Navy leadership as to the relative importance of any particular program—what to fund and what to cut.

We designed the structure to build interaction and consensus. The matrix forces staff members whose focus earlier had been almost exclusively vertical to talk with and compete with each other directly. Before, staff members had talked to their subordinates and superiors within the same office, but rarely to their peers, who worked within another vertical channel associated with another warfare or support area. The earlier process was a wonderful example of stovepipe dialogue, a term that aptly captured the flow of information upward within prescribed channels at the expense of flows across offices within the Navy staff.

The older, vertically oriented process tended to restrict consensus within the staff on general priorities, not only because it limited the flow of information on which consensus depends, but also because it forced interaction across warfare areas to be conducted at higher levels. Even in periods of relative budgetary largess, the competition for funding was fierce, and in the old process only the most senior members of the staff could determine program priorities and make the trade-offs—usually under the intense pressure of schedule deadlines and often without realizing the full implications of such trade-offs because the program officers pushing the disparate programs had never talked to one another.

The new structure, however, forced a horizontal flow of information and rewarded awareness of competing programs. Program advocates were forced to work with other advocates to arrive at an overall sense of program priorities for each of the new mission areas. To acquire what he believed was adequate funding, a submarine advocate, for example, had to convince competitors that his programs contributed more than theirs did to joint littoral warfare, joint strike, and the rest of the mission areas. If he was successful in getting his programs ranked relatively high in each of the mission areas, the probability of funding those programs during the investment balance review increased. To win in this arena, the advocate had to know enough about competing programs and the views of other advocates to demonstrate, objectively, why it was better to fund his programs than others.

This is where the new mission-area titles came in. We dropped older terms—strike, antisubmarine, antiair, and antisurface warfare—largely to free thought and discussion from the definition and intellectual boundaries that had grown up around those terms and replaced them with categories chosen to introduce a joint, broader, more national perspective to Navy programming. As the titles indicate, the standards against which the naval force programs were to be ranked went beyond a parochial Navy vocabulary and focus. The assessment process required its participants to demonstrate the importance of their programs in terms of how they would contribute to joint military operations.

We picked these categories for particular reasons. On the one hand, they provided a potential means of identifying, from an overall naval perspective, the least dangerous funding reductions. The appellation of joint to the mission areas required the staff not only to build an awareness of one another's advocacy and arguments, but also to learn what the other military services could and would want to do in each of them. We used the terms to build an understanding of what resources the Army or Air Force could apply to the given mission area so that the Navy might not have to. They helped identify money going to redundant naval programs we could shift to more important naval force requirements.

The process went beyond attempts to identify potential savings by eliminating redundancies. We also saw it as a means of relating the professed goal of the Navy's new operational concept of "enabling and enhancing the application of joint military force in littoral areas" to the size and structure of naval forces, thereby giving tangible expression to the rhetoric of the new concept. Doing this required the various program sponsors to deal with the concept of force synergism. They had to demonstrate how their programs would assist nonnaval force components in joint military operations—and to rank systems, weapons, and naval forces not only in terms of their contributions to traditional naval warfare tasks, but also in terms of how they would assist the Air Force and the Army in carrying out their missions.

This was new in military force planning. Traditionally, the interest in a joint perspective had been the purview of the Office of the Secretary of Defense and, more recently, the Chairman of the Joint Chiefs of Staff—agencies external to the services—who reviewed service requests for research and acquisition in terms of whether they duplicated another service's programs. The new assessment process in the Navy sought to internalize a joint perspective within a single service's planning process. It forced program advocates to gain an understanding of how the other military services intended to fight. Program advocates were successful in getting their program desires funded to the extent that they could explain how what they advocated would assist another service in combat. Program funding within the Navy depended, at least in part, on how well it contributed to the operational effectiveness of the Army and Air Force.

The new assessment process began in September 1992 and ran through the late summer of 1993. September turned out to be a fortuitous starting point—by the end of January 1993 we could tell how to adjust the Navy's fiscal year 1994 budget request to conform with the new Clinton administration's desires, and by midsummer we could specify the Navy's views on priorities and adjustments for the fiscal year 1995 budget. It seems better in retrospect, however, than it did at the time. It was an unusual event for a bureaucracy, self-initiated by the Navy, not in response to direct tasking by the Secretary of Defense or any other external authority, at a time when the presidential campaign was entering the home stretch. The incumbent administration did not want any leaks that its base force was under review inside the Pentagon, and yet we had begun the new assessment process by hoping and believing that it would, in fact, generate a Navy program that was going to be considerably different from what the base force defined as necessary. We were after a consensus that had teeth, one we could express in specific program priorities that would meet the demands of the new strategy and remain affordable even in the face of declining defense budgets.

This aspect of the assessment process was conducted under the auspices of a board, of which I was chairman, entitled the Resources, Requirements Review Board. The board consisted of the chairmen of each of the Joint Mission Area Assessments—mostly rear admirals—plus Marine Corps general officers and other flag officers from the Navy staff. Representative boards are nothing new to military staff work in Washington, but what distinguished this one was its intensity. We met three times a week in long sessions that featured very open and candid discussions. The involvement of flag officers in the assessment process was remarkable. It became the most demanding, in terms of time and concentration, of all the tasks facing the senior members of the Navy staff.

In a relatively short period, the assessment process generated

—a new force structure target,
—a new sense of program priorities, and
—a new Navy budget target considerably below the one previously submitted for the 1994–99 fiscal year defense plan.

In retrospect, however, the assessment process's most important contribution was to provide the forum and framework for the discussions that led to the first full consensus on the questions raised by the end of the Cold War: what the role of naval forces was to be in the future, and how those forces were to be sized, shaped, and structured. It gave substance to the rhetoric about what the end of the Cold War meant and in doing so began to complete the intellectual transition that had begun with the collapse of the Soviet Union.

All this might have evolved without the staff reorganization and without the joint-mission-area assessment process. But it would not have occurred as soon, and the consensus would not have been as broadly held inside the Navy's leadership or shared as early by senior Defense Department officials and Congress. The assessment process was widely perceived, inside and outside the Navy, as legitimate, honest, objective, and productive—and so were its results.

THE CONSENSUS: THE FUTURE NAVY

The results constituted agreement on how the Navy would change and what it would become over the next two decades—a smaller, technically advanced force, recapitalized for the future, and shaped to meet the implications of joint military operations in littoral areas of the world. Although it will be a smaller force than called for by the base force, it will remain powerful if we maintain and extend the leverage that

Author, left, with Rear Adm. Tom Ryan and Rear Adm. Riley Mixson aboard the USS *Saratoga*. Ryan and Mixson would later be members of the "band of brothers" that made up the first Resources, Requirements Review Board (R3B) in OPNAV.

advanced technology offers us. That is the key. The essence of the consensus pounded out during the first year of the Navy's new assessment process was to emphasize and take advantage of what has come to be called the military technical revolution.

Capitalizing on the Military Technical Revolution

The term "military technical revolution" gained prominence a decade ago largely because the writer claiming he had coined it happened to be Chief of the Soviet General Staff, Marshal of the Soviet Union Yuri Ogarkov. Writing in the 1980s, Marshal Ogarkov was concerned that the United States was moving far ahead of the Soviets in what was loosely called information technology. Whether Ogarkov's insight contributed to his eventual demotion or not is difficult to say. In any event, through the 1980s and into this decade, military theorists in the East and West refined the meaning of the military technical revolution: an improved technical capacity to understand and react to military situations better and faster than an opponent is the key to the successful use of force.[1] This understanding of the term is what we wanted to incorporate into the naval forces of the future. It involves four technical-operational concepts:

—Omniscience based on advanced surveillance and target-acquisition systems and technologies;

—Synergistic integration based on advanced C3I systems;

—Immune power projection based on a family of standoff, precision-guided weapons, as well as space and electronic-warfare capabilities, and ballistic-missile defenses;

—Battlefield support based on new means of providing fire support from the sea, close air support, and a communications and intelligence system that allows naval forces a better perspective on and understanding of ground-force operations.

Omniscience is an exaggeration, of course, for we will never be all-knowing. We should strive to know as much as we can about potential opponents, as well as the conditions that spawn their opposition and condition their actions. To the extent that we move toward omniscience regarding these considerations, however, we will be better able to·deter actions we wish to prevent and, if deterrence fails, to deny aggressors the spoils of their actions, correct the situation their aggression creates, and exact retribution for what they have done. Knowledge alone cannot accomplish this, but coupled with military force, it can lead to success without prohibitive losses.

The concept is not new. Military theorists from Sun Tzu to Clausewitz have pointed out the value of understanding one's enemies and the geographical-political-social context in which they operate. What is different, however, is that some technologies—available either now or soon—will give the United States an edge that approaches omniscience, at least relative to any potential opponents. The technologies include space-based surveillance systems; optical and other electromagnetic sensors; a computer-based capacity to sort, correlate, and interpret data quickly; and the human resources to use the information effectively in making decisions.

Other nations possess or can acquire some of these components. Space-based observation is already available on a commercial basis, and the quality of the images nations can purchase from the French SPOT Image system, or the new Japanese satellites, is improving. Computer technology is available globally, and the United States has no monopoly on bright, dedicated people. Yet few, if any, nations have been able to combine the various components as successfully as the United States. Few, if any, nations have made the kind of investments in these technologies that can significantly reduce the lead the United States currently enjoys in them. Few, if any, nations are as dedicated to developing these technologies. The result is almost certain to be a growing transparency on the part of potential military opponents of the United States in both relative and absolute respects.

To take advantage of these technologies, however, we must continue to develop the command, control, and communications systems needed to convert the intelligence they provide into effective military responses, which is where synergistic integration comes in.

This capability, sometimes referred to as the third stage of the military technological revolution, has been growing rapidly over the last decade. In part, it stemmed from the transition toward omniscience, for as the amounts of data mushroom from space-, atmospheric-, land-, and ocean-based sensors, we face the problem of data overload. By the late 1970s, U.S. military forces in general, and the Navy in particular, were developing ways of handling the growing amounts of available data cooperatively. The United States began to cope with information overload by distributing it among interconnected forces that, working together, could solve complex military problems.

Perhaps one of the best examples was the way the United States sought to solve the problem posed by growing numbers of quieter Soviet submarines. As Soviet submarines grew more sophisticated and quiet through the 1970s, the United States increasingly turned to a global, interconnected team effort to track them. We integrated information from satellites and fixed seabed sensors, which could provide warning of Soviet submarine departures from their bases, with other data, and distributed it among U.S. surface, submarine, and airborne platforms. These, in turn, coordinated their actions, maintaining a nearly constant, integrated flow of data and intelligence among the forces assigned to tracking the submarines—an approach that increasingly produced accurate, real-time location data on the submarines. All U.S. military services developed similar total-force integration in response to a broad spectrum of other military problems.

The capability rested on two kinds of technologies: reliable communications systems able to pass huge amounts of data, information, and intelligence among the units quickly, assisted by computers and software that could process the data quickly. Combining the two provided a leap in the capacity to coordinate complex military operations and was a harbinger of the way the United States was able to operate in Desert Storm.

Coalition land, sea, and air operations in the Gulf War were not so complex as other military campaigns and did not involve as many personnel, but never had so many forces been so coordinated as effectively by means of real-time command and control. The Normandy invasion during World War II involved complex movements of huge forces, but their movements were orchestrated primarily by planning the precise movements of specific forces beforehand and then training the forces accordingly. Once launched, the success of the invasion rested entirely on the adequacy of the planning and the capacity of the forces to do what they had trained so long and hard to do. As Gen. Dwight D. Eisenhower, the Supreme Allied Commander, made clear in his memoirs, the fate of the operation rested on how well it had been planned. Once it was under way, he and the other senior commanders could only watch.

Operations in Desert Storm differed, not because there was a relative lack of planning and training, but because they were managed in real time. Coalition command, control, and communications permitted commanders to take full advantage of the enemy's relative transparency and, in modern military parlance, work within the decision-making cycle of the Iraqi opponent. We knew what the Iraqis were doing before they could do it and, accordingly, could bring our forces to bear against gaps and weaknesses in the opposing forces so as to defeat the opponent's military strategy.

The third component in the Navy's procurement and design planning—immune power projection—is in a sense the cutting edge of the technological revolution. We might defeat any military opponent if we had the first two components. That is, if we had accurate knowledge of the opponent and of the engagement situation, and if we had the command, control, and communications systems sufficient to translate that knowledge into effective military action, we could probably defeat the opponent with the kind of weapons the United States had half a century ago. The costs of doing so, in casualties, time, and money, however, would be high, perhaps prohibitively high. The capacity of a bayonet to kill an opponent is high; the chances of killing an opponent with a bayonet without being endangered are low. The United States and other democracies are understandably reluctant to apply military force if it carries with it the prospect of heavy casualties—a factor potential opponents are well aware of and may use to prevent U.S. intervention. But if the United States can apply military force with impunity, we may not have to use force at all: the threat of intervening militarily may be sufficient to forestall aggression.

The basic principle underlying the Navy's force-structuring strategy, then, is to be able to apply military force quickly, with great effectiveness, and in such a way as to minimize the risk to the military personnel applying force. We believe this requires strong emphasis on a system of intelligence, targeting systems, battle-damage-assessment systems, and standoff weapons that can destroy targets quickly and precisely without exposing our forces to danger. The effectiveness of such systems, of course, rests on our capacity to develop omniscience and synergistic integration. The use of standoff, precision weapons must be based on knowledge of potential opponents sufficient to identify and target those things that are key to their military capabilities and operational schemes, and on the capacity of the integrated command, control, and communications systems to carry out coordinated attacks on time. If we can develop these two components fully, we will achieve the full potential of the weapons we plan to give to naval forces.

The notion of a family of such weapons is worth a final comment. We cannot bet on developing and fielding a single standoff weapon in the hope that it will turn out to be precisely the one needed. Nor should we try to develop a multipurpose weapon that can meet all the demands of future conflict. The first approach surpasses our ability to foretell the future; the second would break the bank. What we need is a family of weapons that, together,

—give naval forces the ability to strike targets at varying ranges, and
—employ different sensors and guidance systems that provide an all-weather capability in varying environments and that we can employ from different platforms.

It is not necessary that these weapons be developed or used solely by U.S. naval forces. In fact, we plan to develop and field them in concert with the Army and the Air Force and, perhaps, our allies. Such an approach is more than cost-effective; it supports the Navy's new emphasis on enabling joint-military-force operations.

Battlefield support is the final part of the equation. Here, also, certain military technologies and a way of thinking about their use are keys to the concept. At the most obvious level, battlefield support involves better ways of doing some things naval forces have done in the past. Providing fire support for troops landing or operating ashore, for example, is a tactical tradition of long standing. Because of its focus on directly affecting events on land, naval surface fire support is of particular interest in the new operational concept. What we want to build into our forces, then, is the ability to deliver fire from the sea and provide close air support with the greater precision, timeliness, and effectiveness offered by the new technologies. We intend to incorporate smart weapons into this effort and to do so in innovative, cost-effective ways that take advantage of what the Army and Air Force have already developed or are working on. The Army, for example, has developed a ballistic missile that can deliver sensor-fused weapons against armored forces on the move at ranges of up to 175 miles. This is the kind of capability that fits well with our interest in battlefield support, and we intend to add it to naval platforms.

At a deeper level, however, the interest in battlefield support goes to how we think naval forces should view naval operations. In effect, we must add the view from the foxhole to that perception. We must instill a sense of ground operational priorities and concerns into our naval forces. In part, this requires an ability to tap into the information and intelligence flows used by the Army and the Marines and to pass our information and intelligence to them in forms they can use. It also involves a long-term learning process that includes operating and living jointly, for it is something that can be acquired only with experience.

Two Steps to the Future

It is helpful to envision the movement toward the future Navy in terms of two steps. The first step, which we call Force 2001, represents what we can do with the weapons, systems, and platforms that are already here or on the way. In a general sense, Force 2001 reflects how we intend to adjust today's force to meet the demands of the operational concepts implied by joint military operations in the littoral. It will differ from what exists today in many respects, but the fact remains that many of the ships, weapons, and systems that are in the present force will also be present seven years from now. In any event, we could not develop and deploy a radically different Navy by 2001 even if we wanted to.

Force 2001, therefore, ought to be seen as a first step; it is an interim force on the way to a Navy that will be very different from today's. The second step might be called Force 2021. This force will be the product not only of evolutionary changes but of the culmination of the new concepts we plan to introduce today.

Why talk about a force that will not exist for more than two decades? One reason has to do with how long it takes to incorporate conceptual change into tangible results. Historically, it has taken a decade or more for new ship and systems designs to enter active military service, after which they normally serve for decades. Accordingly, 2021 is the year that ideas the Navy is now beginning to incorporate into its planning will reach fruition. While the force that emerges a quarter century from now will undoubtedly be different from what we project it to be today— and the Navy has consciously built flexibility into its ships and aircraft to allow modifications and improvements—thinking about the future implications of what we are doing today helps us to understand and evaluate today's actions.

Chapter 7

Force 2001

One expression of the new consensus was Force 2001, the force we believe the Navy should move toward over the remainder of this decade. The structure, composition, and capabilities of this force are best seen as a target, built from judgments we made during the assessment process. We recognized that the specific numbers and kinds of ships that will make up the turn-of-the-century Navy may not be the same as the ones we envisioned. But we would be surprised if Force 2001 differed radically from the target we devised in 1993.

DEFINING HOW MUCH IS ENOUGH

How much is enough? The answer, of course, is another rhetorical question: "Enough for what?"

In the past, there was a consensus, inside and outside the Defense Department, about how to deal with these tough questions, for everyone recognized that as long as the nation's survival was at stake, it made a great deal of sense to spend whatever was necessary to reduce the risk. Since there was also a general consensus on what constituted that risk—Soviet military power—there was general agreement on the template to determine how much U.S. defense was enough. This hardly ended heated debate over the specific levels or types of military forces that were necessary, nor how much the nation ought to spend on building those forces. Everyone worked from similar sheets of music, however, and the result was generally harmonious, even though punctuated by sometimes extended passages of cacophony.

When Secretary of Defense Robert McNamara first posed the question, how much was enough for defense, he also supplied a working answer: "Whatever was necessary for the defense of the United States, and no more." This was an explicit recognition, first, of the national priority attached to national defense and, second, that we ought to spend the money efficiently. The substance of the formula today, however, is different. For one thing, how we define the dangers to the nation has changed. Those dangers, for example, now explicitly include the idea that we should not plan forces, or demand the money necessary to build force levels, that increase the risk of eroding the nation's relative economic standing.

This idea has always been around, but now it is explicit, and making it explicit elevates the requirement to spend money efficiently, which should be obvious. Yet as long as Americans believed the survival of their nation was imminently at risk, they tended to subordinate the interest in efficiency to the larger goal of spending whatever was necessary to assure the nation's survival in the face of a deadly threat. The priorities now accorded resource allocation, however, have created additional pressures to innovate—because the defense budget is going down.

Two general considerations go into calculating how much is enough. The first is the "war-fighting" requirement: that is, what we think we need to win two major regional conflicts. That depends on many judgments—how demanding such conflicts might be, where they would take place, and when they might begin are only starting points. This can get pretty esoteric, so it is important to remember that the different scenarios used in such calculations are simply a way of coming up with a reasonable, systematic answer to the question of how much the nation needs for the kinds of conflicts it might face in the years ahead.

Navy planners also try to build forces that reduce the likelihood that we will have to fight wars. Secretary of Defense Aspin made this point in testimony before the Senate Armed Forces Committee in 1993, when he argued, "Our naval forces should be sized and shaped not only for armed conflict, but also for the myriad of other important tasks we call upon them to do. Forward presence is certainly a key ingredient of this mix, along with such missions as peacekeeping, humanitarian assistance, deterrence and crisis control."[1]

War-Fighting Requirements

War-fighting requirements—what we need to win wars—obviously depend on the kinds of wars anticipated. It is fairly complicated because you have to use assumptions about future capabilities on both sides; because wars are always high-stakes events, you do not want whatever calculations you use to define force requirements to err on the side of too little. Finally, war-fighting requirements get wrapped into the issue of deterrence because you would prefer to deter the war you anticipate.

Military planners, however, are not paid to philosophize endlessly about the complexities and difficulties of defining force requirements for potential conflicts—they are charged with presenting clear statements of what they believe those requirements are, and an intelligent set of reasons to support their conclusions. Doing this is really only an early step because a lot of groups other than the military have much to say about what the nation ultimately defines as its war-fighting requirements. It is an important step, though, and military planners expend an enormous amount of effort in trying to do it well.

One logical approach is to use a planning scenario, a hypothetical conflict with specific statements about where, when, and how it would take place and who would be involved. The scenarios are not really predictions of the conflicts the United States will face, but they conform to what most would accept as a reasonably possible event. A few years ago the dominant planning scenario portrayed a worldwide war with another military superpower, the Soviet Union. Now, the Defense Department uses several major regional contingencies as planning scenarios and charges each military service to identify what it needs to win two major regional contingencies that occur more or less simultaneously in different parts of the world.

The Navy believes the United States must be able to assemble quickly up to ten Naval Expeditionary Task Forces and to maintain them in combat. This number represents a prudent risk capability; some combinations of regional contingencies would require more than this, but the Department of Defense believes those contingencies are unlikely enough so that military planners can ignore them in calculating war-fighting requirements for the forces of the future. The notional level of ten NETFs does not represent the total inventory of ships, aircraft, and other systems that must be available to meet requirements, particularly at short notice. Some of the ships making up the war-fighting requirement would be deployed overseas relatively close to the contingency; others might not.

Historically, for example, roughly 15 percent of the active-ship inventory is in overhaul at any given time and could require up to a year to come on line. Other ships might be undergoing maintenance and so would not be available immediately. To maintain the level of force required for the duration of the two regional conflicts, especially if we cannot end the conflicts in a relatively short time, we may need additional ships to fill in gaps created by battle damage. We might have to withhold other ships from the conflict to assure capability to respond to minor crises that may erupt elsewhere during the conflicts, or to support other operations within the region, such as protecting the sea lines of communication. The time required to rotate ships to and from the regional contingency also has an effect on the overall requirement.

All of these considerations can be expressed as an "availability factor," which differs for each class of ship, or a "withhold factor." Both of these factors come from historical data and probability estimates. Adding these factors to the calculations of the war-fighting requirement provides the total number of ships, aircraft, and other systems that would have to be in the Navy's inventory in order to meet the requirements of the planning scenarios. In terms of the surface-combatant requirements, for example, the calculations look something like table 7:1 for the ten NETFs required by the planning scenarios.

TABLE 7:1 Surface Combatants Required by Two Major Regional Contingencies

On Station in Conflict*	Plus	Availability Factor	Plus	Withhold Factor	Equals	Total Required
85–115	+	14–15	+	15	=	114–45

*Calculated on the basis of numbers associated with NETGs involved in two simultaneous contingencies, and additional functions such as combat search and rescue, and maritime-interdiction operations.

Presence Requirements

The forces needed for overseas presence reflect the assumptions made about where, when, and how the United States will want to maintain overseas presence in the future. These are at least as difficult to predict as forecasting when and where wars will break out, but it is reasonable to expect that, at least for the remainder of this century, the United States will want to maintain a continual military presence in Europe, Southwest Asia, the Pacific, and Latin America. The demands of overseas presence in these areas are likely to fall increasingly on the nation's naval forces, particularly as U.S. land-based forces pull back to the United States.

The forward-presence requirement is important in determining naval force levels because overseas deployments are active undertakings. They mean days at sea, and days at sea equate to constant operations, wearing down sailors and machines. Meeting the demands of overseas presence, therefore, requires more assets than simply the number of ships on station overseas at any given time.

This is why the Navy talks about a rotation base, which is a function of what it takes to cover the transit times from home ports to deployment areas and the preparation and training required to withstand the rigors of months at sea on peacetime deployments. This usually requires

The USS *Abraham Lincoln* operating in the Indian Ocean. The number of carriers needed is a function of both war-fighting and presence requirements. (U.S. Navy)

more than one ship in the rotation base—in the pipeline, if you will—for every ship that is on station overseas. We can calculate the number needed by using a factor that encompasses transit times (assuming overseas home porting where that is available), maintenance scheduling, overhauls, the preferred length of a peacetime deployment, and all the other variables involved.

Table 7:2, focusing on surface combatants, illustrates how we estimate the number of ships needed to maintain a continuous presence in various areas.

THE SHAPE OF THE NAVY TO COME

These two examples of how we go about determining force levels—warfighting requirements and presence requirements—end up with similar numbers for surface combatants. In each case, of course, the numbers generated are sensitive to many assumptions that could change. Mod-

TABLE 7:2 Notional Continuous Peacetime Presence for Four World Areas

Area of Concern	Force Configuration	Surface Combatants	Rotation Base Factor	Total Needed Inventory
Southwest	CV NETG	4	6.8	27
Asia	LHA/D NETG	2	6.8	14
	NETU[a]	3	6.8	21
Europe	CV NETG	3	4.2	12
	LHA/D NETG	2	4.2	8
	NETE[b]	1	4.0	4
	NETE[c]	1	3.8	4
Pacific	CV NETG	3–4	2.0	6–8
	LHA/D NETG	2	2.0	4
Latin	NETU[d]	2–4	2.0	4–8
America	NETU[e]	2	2.0	8
				112–18

[a]Middle East Task Unit
[b]Standing NATO Force, Mediterranean
[c]Standing NATO Force Atlantic
[d]Counter-Drug Operations
[e]UNITAS

ernization and innovation in the way we operate the combatants can produce higher combat outputs—which means that we might be able to meet the war-fighting requirement with fewer ships. New synergism with forces provided by the other services could do the same thing. Adjusting the way we conduct overseas deployments could have similar effects on presence requirements.

Given the financial constraints we expect in the future, we will have to balance ship-requirement calculations carefully. All of these considerations, and others, played on Navy planning from the fall of 1992 through the summer of 1993. Table 7:3 portrays the results. It compares projected levels under Force 2001 with the forces that existed in 1988, the year the Navy reached the six hundred–ship level—and the year that our active ship inventory began its downward slant. Force 2001 assumes we will continue to build fewer ships; by the beginning of the next century we expect to have roughly half the number of ships the Navy had shortly before the Soviet Union collapsed. We also expect to reach a plateau at about 330 ships overall at about the turn of the century.

The largest reductions will occur in submarines and in surface combatants; the smallest in amphibious lift and supercarriers. The numbers of mine-countermeasure ships will actually increase modestly. Force 2001 will not be simply a smaller version of the force we have today—it will be different, and its ships will reflect the transition from a sea-control Navy toward a Navy better structured to project power from the sea

TABLE 7:3 Force 2001 Comparison

	1988	2001	Reduction
Total Active Ships	600	320–50	47–42%
Total Manpower	526,000	375,000–400,000	24%
Surface Combatants	194	110–16	43%
Minesweepers	4	16	400% increase
Combat Logistics	58	47 (35 MSC manned)	10%
Other Support Ships	66	35	47%
Supercarriers	14	12	14%
Air Wings	15	11	26%
Tactical Aircraft per Wing	55	50+	8%
Amphibious Lift	2.5 MEB	2.5 MEB	none
	52 ships	35 ships	33%
SSNs	100	55	47%
SSBNs	30	18	41%

to the land. That shift toward power projection is in part a function of maintaining amphibious-lift capabilities at a relatively high level and increasing the numbers of mine-detection and -countermeasures platforms and systems. We are talking about a force that is smaller than what we have today but that is in some respects more potent, particularly in the context of the littoral warfare we believe will remain the focus of U.S. maritime strategy well into the next century.

Recapitalization

To get a fuller sense of what Force 2001 will be, however, it is necessary to do more than just count ships. Beneath the obvious trends of reduced numbers and a shift in the mix of ships lies a more general strategy of recapitalization. Two aspects of the strategy are of special importance. The first is that we will not maintain platforms in the active-ship inventory that deliver only marginal war-fighting utility relative to their cost to operate and maintain. In the days of plentiful budgets and the drive to reach a six hundred–ship Navy, this consideration was quite muted—but no longer. The first aspect of recapitalization, then, means paring the force structure with the criteria of cost-effectiveness.

The second aspect is a logical extension of the first: how we apply some of the savings generated in the first step. We want to buy new platforms that incorporate the latest in war-fighting and engineering technology. We intend to move toward a more modern, capable force as we

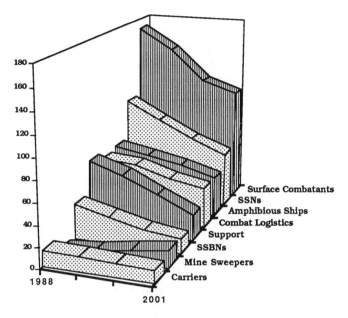

FIGURE 7:1 The Shape of the Navy to Come

reduce the number of active-duty ships, even if that means decommissioning some ships that have considerable service life left. We will do this within the constraints of a declining budget because we will decommission more ships than we build; the tradeoff for the period 1995 to 1999 will be on the order of three decommissionings for every new build. The fleet will become more technologically advanced, and the newer ships will help us avoid block obsolescence and also contribute to preserving an industrial base. That is, we have chosen a strategy to avoid a future situation in which large numbers of ships arrive at the end of their service life together, and the Navy finds itself without the funds or the shipyard capacity to rectify the problem.

Recapitalization means the Navy will not keep a force structure that it cannot maintain properly and upgrade to the standards that will be required for modern warships. We believe those standards stress high modernization and high readiness. We want to invest every year with that in mind, buying enough ships to recapitalize our forces continuously. Force 2001 is the level at which we can do this.

The recapitalization will feature a technological drive toward omniscience, synergistic integration, immune power projection, and support for the ground battlefield. Whereas Force 2001 will in some respects look like a smaller version of today's force, an important metamorphosis will be under way by the end of the decade. By 2000, for example, an NETF, however organized and deployed, will carry up to five hundred standoff weapons capable of striking fixed targets at ranges of one thousand miles with great accuracy. That same NETF will have one thousand times more capability to communicate than it has today. It will be able to attack enemy armored and motorized forces with sensor-fuzed weapons, and because of the advances in surveillance and C3I, it will be able to do this quickly, in the context of rapidly evolving operations in support of friendly ground forces.

The second underlying trend is the focus on developing platforms and systems that are far more capable of effective joint operations in littoral areas. This is a function not only of shifts in the mix of ships, but also of changes in the way we think about using the new, technologically advanced ships and systems.

Building a Littoral-Warfare Surface Component

Over the remainder of this decade, we intend to decommission several classes of surface ships and, as the *Arleigh Burke* (DDG 51) –class ships enter the force, shift the character of the surface-combatant component of Force 2001 to fewer, more capable multipurpose platforms. Nuclear-powered cruisers, 1052-class frigates, hydrofoil patrol ships, and the CG 16/27 cruisers will leave, and the *Oliver Hazard Perry* (FFG 7) –class frigates will be on their way out by the end of the decade.

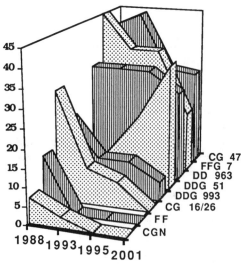

FIGURE 7:2 The Shape of the Surface Force to Come

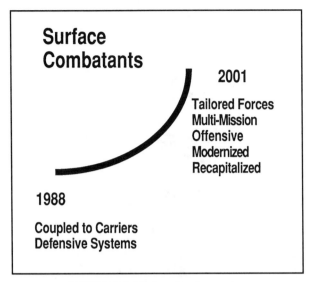

FIGURE 7:3 Surface Combatants

We will transfer surface ships optimized for and basically limited to antisubmarine-warfare roles from the active forces to the reserves. The surface-combatant force that emerges will be composed largely of Aegis-capable platforms, all of which can be upgraded to provide theater-ballistic-missile defenses from the sea over the land. It will carry a potent long-range, land-attack capability in the form of improved Tomahawk land-attack missiles. It will have much better naval surface fire-support capabilities. The mine-countermeasures force will increase to roughly 10 percent of the total number of ships. Overall, as figure 7:3 suggests, we want to move away from investing in relatively large numbers of smaller ships. We do not anticipate a requirement to protect the sea lanes against interdiction by another sea power, and thus it is illogical to maintain frigates that were built to escort convoys. As the growth in the numbers of DDG 51s indicates, we intend to move toward more capable, multipurpose surface platforms.

In a broad sense, then, we will move toward a surface force optimized for littoral warfare and one increasingly capable of projecting power across the littoral onto land. We will not abandon fleet defense, for that basic requirement will continue through the transition to a full focus on fighting in the littorals. We do plan to shift the primary focus of the surface-warfare component of Force 2001 toward warfare in the littoral with an emphasis on long-range strike, primarily through advanced versions of the Tomahawk land-attack cruise missile; battlefield support,

The USS *Arleigh Burke*–class DDG 51 will form the core of the surface force for the rest of this century. (Bath Iron Works)

possibly to include incorporating the Army tactical missile system (ATACMS) aboard surface ships; and an ability to provide regional air and ballistic-missile defenses across a region.

Sea-Based Ballistic-Missile Defenses

Current planning calls for a two-step process in building the sea-based ballistic-missile-defense system. The first step would be to obtain a lower-tier area-defense capability by 1997. This would be done primarily with software changes that allow the Aegis SPY radar to search at longer range and higher altitude. It would also involve modifying the warhead, fuze, and seeker of the improved Standard Missile (SM-2 Block IVA) to give it a better capability against incoming warheads. These modifications would give the Aegis-equipped ships an endoatmospheric ballistic-missile-intercept capability.

The second step, which could be taken by about 1999, would result in an exoatmospheric intercept capability. Sometimes referred to as an upper-tier theater-wide capability, we can achieve this in part by adding a new stage—perhaps the Lightweight Exoatmospheric Projectile (LEAP)—to the Standard Missile (SM-2 Block IVA) or by modifying the Army's Theater High Altitude Area Defense (THAAD) missile for launch from shipborne Aegis vertical-launch tubes.

In either tier, the success of a sea-based missile-defense system will depend on our ability to employ remote sensors to cue the Aegis ship onto the incoming missiles while they are beyond the ship's radar horizon. The remote sensors may be space-based, but they could also include airborne or ground-based systems. Such cuing would allow the Aegis fire-control radar to focus its energy in the area of the incoming trajectory, thus extending the range at which it could detect, track, and direct the engagement of the target. This, in turn, would allow intercept of the incoming missile at greater distances from the ship.

The cuing would result in an engagement range of six hundred miles or more for the upper-tier capability and an engagement range of more than sixty miles for the lower-tier capability. Assuming the Aegis-equipped ship was close to shore, the lower-tier capability would allow the sea-based ballistic-missile-defense system to provide the kind of area defense that would cover virtually any port area or airfield to a range of about sixty miles. The upper-tier capability would be able to extend that umbrella over virtually an entire region. The sea-based missile-defense system envisioned in these plans is not intended to compete with land-based theater-ballistic-missile defenses like the Army's THAAD. On the contrary, it can work synergistically with such systems along the lines suggested in the earlier discussion of joint operations.

Naval Aviation: Integrated Power Projection and Ground-Support Force

We predicated Force 2001 on maintaining a powerful carrier force. Although it will have fewer large aircraft carriers than we do today, we will keep the number necessary to meet the demands of major regional military contingencies and to meet the additional demands of overseas presence. The major change in the carrier force will be what they carry.

We expect the carrier-aviation component of Force 2001 to be a transitional step on the way to a much more eclectic view of naval air power, one that emphasizes tailoring the mix of aircraft on the carriers to the anticipated tasks, and one that accepts the notion of surging additional aircraft and aircrews—or aircrews alone—to the carriers in times of need. This promises big payoffs in savings and is but one example of how the drive for efficiency at lower costs can help stimulate innovation.

The carrier's aircraft will be more capable of supporting battlefield operations than is the case today. This shift will be driven, so far as Force 2001 is concerned, by a number of incremental changes to the aircraft that will compose that force, and by the introduction of a new family of air-delivered precision-guided weapons. By the turn of the century, F/A-18E/F aircraft will be entering the operational inventory. These longer-range models will deliver standoff, precision-guided, and sensor-fused weapons much more efficiently than is possible with the F/A-18C/D aircraft in the fleet today. We will also modify the remaining F-14s to give this capable fighter a significantly better ground-attack capability. Taken as a whole, Force 2001 will shift the Navy's aircraft toward modern, more effective multipurpose attack and air-to-air capabilities.

We will make the aircraft improvements in parallel with a strong push toward a family of standoff weapons. These include accurate midrange precision strike capability in the form of an improved Standoff Land Attack Missile (SLAM), the Tri-Service Standard Attack Missile

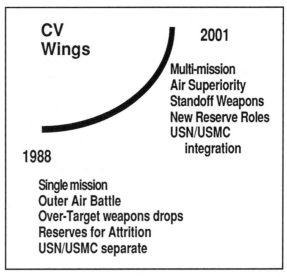

FIGURE 7:4 CV Wings

(TSSAM) for delivery by carrier-based aircraft, and the Joint Standoff Weapon (JSOW), now under development. We intend to put together a flexible, integrated air-strike and -bombardment capability that will work as an integral part of any joint military operation.

Better communications will help build that capability. We will improve the near- and overland capabilities of the aircraft we use for surveillance and extend their ability to communicate with Air Force AWACS aircraft and other systems involved in joint military operations, regardless of the military service that provides them. Although naval aviation will be able to provide the nation with an independent strike capability of impressive range, quick response, destructive potential, and precision, it will also be much better able to operate as an integral, synergistic component of any U.S. joint military operation.

A More Powerful Amphibious and Land-Combat Support Force

Paralleling the trend associated with surface combatants, the amphibious forces of Force 2001 will consist of fewer but more capable ships. We expect the overall amphibious capability to improve even though the numbers of amphibious-operations ships will decline.

We will put much of the improved capability into the *Tarawa* (LHA 1) and *Wasp* (LHD 1) -class amphibious-assault ships. These vessels—as large as World War II *Essex* (CV 9) -class aircraft carriers—are flexible platforms with a broad range of capabilities. We plan to make these

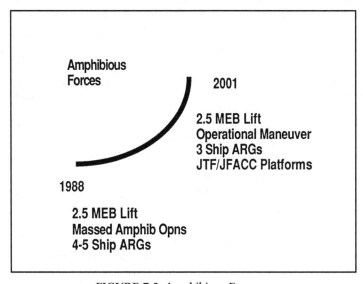

FIGURE 7:5 Amphibious Forces

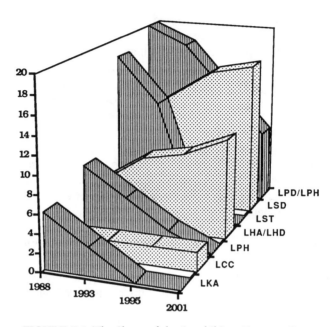

FIGURE 7:6 The Shape of the Amphibious Force to Come

ships far more versatile than they are now, largely by upgrading their communications capabilities, making them, in effect, seaborne command centers capable of providing the command, control, and communications necessary to conduct joint operations. The LHAs and LHDs at the center of the amphibious component of Force 2001 will emerge as both an amphibious and a land-combat-support force, capable of delivering significant land-combat power over the shore quickly and of controlling and supporting joint combat operations involving not just Navy and Marine forces but also Army and Air Force components.

The Shape of the Amphibious Force to Come

Those same communications capabilities, and new radar-equipped, night-attack AV-8B Harrier STOVL aircraft, will change the view that these ships are restricted to supporting amphibious operations. They will become more flexible instruments of naval power, increasingly capable of sea-control missions, particularly when linked with submarines, an Aegis surface ship, and land-based maritime-patrol aircraft. The changes planned for key elements of the amphibious component are typical of the broader design of Force 2001. They represent the conscious and systematic effort to introduce conceptual revolutions in addition to expanded capabilities.

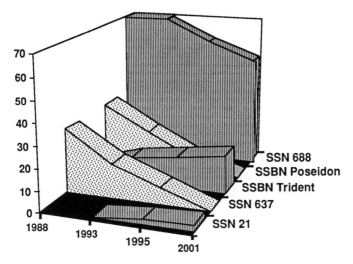

FIGURE 7:7 The Shape of the Submarine Force to Come

Submarine Capabilities for the Future

We plan to reduce the number of nuclear-powered attack submarines (SSNs) dramatically, dropping from the current level of eighty-six SSNs to fifty to fifty-five boats. We will also reduce the numbers of nuclear-powered ballistic-missile submarines (SSBNs) from the current level of thirty—composed of both Poseidon and Trident submarines—to an eighteen-SSBN all-Trident force. By the end of this decade, the United States will have fewer submarines than at any time since before World War II.

The Shape of the Submarine Force to Come

The rate of submarine reductions we anticipate is in part a function of the cost and capacity to dismantle their nuclear power plants safely. Even if there were no costs involved in submarine reductions, however, dismantling the submarine force precipitously would be wrong for two reasons. First, we must maintain powerful sea-control and strategic-nuclear-deterrence capabilities, both because the need has not evaporated and because we must hedge against the future. Second, our submarines will play an important role in littoral warfare, including battlefield support.

The *Ohio* (SSBN 726) -class Tridents are the nation's best platforms for strategic nuclear deterrence. By the turn of the century, the United States may maintain virtually its entire active nuclear arsenal on board

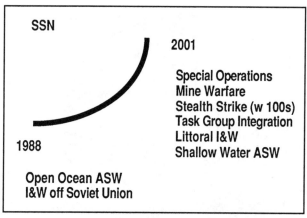

FIGURE 7:8   SSN

these stealthy, survivable submarines. The *Los Angeles* (SSN 688) –class and the new SSN 21 *Seawolf*–class attack submarines will remain the preeminent sea-control platforms, the best submarines in the world for this purpose; and their stealthy surveillance and strike-warfare capabilities also suit them well for battlefield support.

Force 2001 will expand this potential by giving them new technologies. Expanded communications capabilities will play a large role. Technical improvements will permit the submarines to tap into the secure EHF communications networks of the Copernicus communications upgrade, the basis for the general expansion of communications capabilities throughout the fleet. We also will upgrade the surveillance capabilities of the submarines by adding systems that will allow them to monitor all facets of the electromagnetic spectrum, process the data acquired, and provide it immediately to any command node—from the local military-task-force commander to the National Command Authority. We intend to give them the capability to receive such data also.

We will expand the submarine's capabilities to use underwater unmanned vehicles and unmanned aerial vehicles, in the modes outlined in the earlier discussion of undersea operations. These will permit a much greater radius of surveillance and influence, without compromising the submarines' long suit of stealth. In addition to their torpedo tubes, Force 2001 SSNs will have vertical-launch systems that will be capable of launching cruise and other missiles. The challenge, not simple but certainly manageable, is to load those tubes with an appropriate mix of weapons to support the land war.

Broadly speaking, Force 2001 will move toward a submarine force that is more capable of performing three roles: strategic deterrence, sea control, and battlefield support. Force 2001 will promote submarine capabilities that challenge traditional submarine operations and promote new contributions from the submarine force. By 2001, our SSNs will routinely operate in water as shallow as eighty to one hundred feet and will be able to lie on the bottom if necessary. This in-close capability will dramatically expand this stealth vessel's utility in the littoral. This is a conceptual revolution; Force 2001 will allow our submarines to focus directly on land control, while preserving the traditional and still important role of sea control and strategic nuclear deterrence.

GETTING THERE: A REALISTIC FISCAL STRATEGY AND TOUGH CHOICES

The force emerging from the introspection, innovations, and reviews of the last few years comes from an evaluation of what the nation needs, based on the perspective of experienced Navy and Marine Corps leaders. It will be a smaller force than has existed for decades; the target goes down to a level last seen at sea before the Korean War. This is possible because so much has changed over the last several years. The threat has decreased, and the risk these reductions entail is acceptable.

It is important to note, however, that the decisions on the size and shape of the battle force were not driven by any sense that the nation does not need powerful naval forces. The architects of Force 2001 did not believe the nation has any desire to disarm or any intention of relinquishing U.S. maritime superiority. On the contrary, they believed their task was to adjust the nation's naval capabilities to suit a changed world, not to disband. We designed Force 2001 to cope with a future world as we best understood it would be from our 1993 perspective.

Because Force 2001 will be smaller, it will be less expensive. The architects anticipated a declining budget over the remainder of this decade and assumed that the Navy will have to manage annual declines of at least $2–3 billion until then. There are a number of ways to do this, and the military services have had some experience in adjusting to lower budgets. We argued in favor of avoiding some of the ways this has been done in the past.

We thought it best not to bet on the come. We sometimes tried to manage earlier budget reductions on the assumption that the future would eventually deliver larger budgets. The budget strategy that stems from this kind of bettor's hope, however, always turned out to be one that built programs by adding small wedges—slivers of program elements, all of which were there to maintain the chance that when more money was available, they could blossom forth and obtain the capability the full program promised.

Sometimes the bet paid off, but more often it did not, and the result was to push the anticipated fruition further and further into the future, just beyond each year's version of the multiyear defense plan. It was an expensive approach, and one that can lead almost inevitably to a hollow force, subject to massive block obsolescence if the hoped-for surge in funding fails to materialize. It is essentially a dishonest way to do business, particularly if one is serious about controlling the peaks and valleys of defense spending and wants to maintain deterrence over the long run. Unexpected threats that emerge suddenly play havoc with such approaches as the nation is forced to raise budgets precipitously to compensate for frittering away funds on a plethora of programs that never came to fruition before the threat emerged.

We made an important assumption about the future in devising our fiscal strategy to reach Force 2001. We did not plan on an upsurge of money just beyond the current planning period. Instead, we assumed the budget would reach a lower level somewhere around the end of this decade and would remain at that level indefinitely. If we are wrong in this assumption, and the future turns out darker than we now anticipate, we believe the United States will have a force and an industrial-technological base it could expand in time to meet unanticipated threats, because we built a recapitalization process into our force-reduction plans. We rejected the notion that the Navy should plan as if the defense budget will necessarily expand in the future, and we discarded the kind of additive, program-wedge strategy that stems from such an assumption. This required us to make the difficult decisions about cuts now—and we did.

We also thought the Navy should make its force reductions sooner rather than later. This, too, goes against precedent, for the strategy usually adopted in the past to deal with reductions sought the most gradual glide slope across as many years as possible. We did not want to make cuts precipitously, but neither did we wish to extend them artificially because, like betting that the future will certainly provide more money, stretching out reductions is expensive, often leads to imbalances, and assures last-minute cuts that are always more disruptive. Thus, the investment strategy that underlies Force 2001 sought some tough vertical force-structure cuts early to free the resources to build a powerful, technologically advanced, and sustainable smaller force for the future.

The Infrastructure

How did we think we could do it? We believed we could reduce force structure and still recapitalize the force, even on a declining budget, by cutting the naval infrastructure.

An F/A-18 launches a SLAM. Standoff, precision-guided weapons are one of the keys to effective combat operations. (McDonnell Douglas Corp.)

The naval infrastructure today is vast. It is also very important to the nation's naval strength because the nation's naval power flows from what the forces are and from the infrastructure—the industrial facilities, housing and human services, training installations, and other components—that house, train, service, maintain, and repair those forces. If the nation's naval forces are to respond quickly to crises, if they are to maintain their combat edge in peacetime and prevail in conflict, they must be backed and supported by an efficient and effective infrastructure. The nation's military capabilities depend intimately on a balance between forces and infrastructure.

The key here is balance, and the reality is that a proper balance between naval forces and infrastructure does not currently exist. The Navy has today more infrastructure than it needs, one that was built to support a one thousand–ship fleet. The overcapacity is expensive, and maintaining it will put the goal of recapitalizing the force out of reach unless we restore a balance between forces and infrastructure.

Bringing the infrastructure into balance with the force will not be easy. Over the last four decades the military infrastructure has grown deep into the American political and economic systems. Bringing the Navy's portion of that vast network into line with Force 2001 will mean closing base facilities and eliminating jobs whose preservation has, in some cases, become an end in itself. Some of the necessary infrastructure

Increasingly effective surveillance systems, such as the Joint Surveillance and Target Acquisition Radar System, shown here, are another key to combat effectiveness. (Rockwell International)

reduction will take place as the nation goes through the politically difficult process of closing bases. Yet, as we saw it in the summer of 1993, that process was unlikely to move as rapidly or go as deeply as necessary if we were going to be able to recapitalize the force as quickly as required.

As a result, we decided to take a number of initiatives ourselves to reshape the Navy's infrastructure. These include consolidating facilities and using infrastructure elements maintained by other services or local communities. In a broad sense, we will move toward consolidating infrastructure functions—training, maintenance, supply, and all the other activities that go into maintaining the quality of the force—into fewer bases. Force 2001 will ultimately emerge as more than a force structure; it will also size and shape the shore establishment.

AN OVERVIEW: THE STRATEGY-FORCE MATCH

"... From the Sea" marked a conceptual revolution in U.S. naval strategy and called for naval expeditionary forces, shaped for joint operations, that could project U.S. military power forward from the sea. We designed Force 2001 specifically and carefully to meet that goal. It will be an integrated Navy–Marine Corps force, shaped to provide worldwide agility. It will provide sustainable air superiority, strike, and battle-field support where there is no land basing and work effectively with other force components in joint operations. It will offer command, control, communications, and intelligence support for the entire range of joint operations.

There are many paths the Navy might have taken to reach this goal. The one we advocated is not the easiest, but from the nation's perspective, it is arguably the best. We chose in favor of making the force reductions and the concomitant reductions in personnel and, in particular, the infrastructure ashore sooner rather than later. We said the Navy had to maintain the readiness of its fleets and recapitalize them. We said we would build a strong Navy. Real people will have to make real sacrifices, but it is the best course into the high seas of the future.

Chapter 8

Force 2021

We worked hard in that first Strategic Studies Group to determine how the Maritime Strategy could be the final answer to what the Navy should do, and we rarely thought that we would ever face a whole new world. It's humbling when you think about what a difference a few years, let alone a decade or so, can make.

If Force 2001 is a target for the size and shape of the Navy in the relative short run, Force 2021 is essentially speculative. It represents my sense of where the path to Force 2001 could lead if we push the assumptions and implications used in building Force 2001 to their logical conclusions. It is a forecast of things that might be.

There are some general points to be made about the size and shape of naval forces thirty years hence. First, it is important to distinguish the kind of force that could exist three decades in the future from the kind of force that can exist at the end of this decade. Force 2001 will consist almost entirely of ships and aircraft that are already operational or are far enough through the development and procurement process that we know pretty much what they will look like and what they will be able to do. Ships and most modern naval systems are complicated; producing them takes time. On average, it takes about two decades for ships and aircraft to move from the idea stage through design, engineering, production, and testing to operational service with the fleets. Not everything takes that long, but it would be virtually impossible to introduce ships, aircraft, and other major systems in this decade that differ greatly from what exists today or from what we already see coming through the production pipeline.

Force 2021, however, is another matter. It is far enough in the future to include ships and aircraft that could differ greatly from what we see today. Indeed, if the present production process remains more or less similar to what it is today, ships, aircraft, and other naval systems not yet designed will make up much of Force 2021. It could be radically different from today's force and from what we expect Force 2001 to be—or it could be similar. The commanders and lieutenant commanders of today, who will be running the Navy early in the next century, may decide then that Force 2001 ought to last in form and substance through the next two decades. The result by the second decade of the next century would be something that looks like today's force or, rather, an evolutionary development of what we have today. Force 2021 has a wide range of possibilities.

How can we go beyond this platitude? There are, I think, two ways of narrowing the possible into a reasonable forecast of the more likely. One is to look at the kinds of ships, aircraft, and major weapons systems that are on the drawing boards today, and the other is to extend today's ideas and trends to their logical conclusion.

Some of the ships, aircraft, and weapons will move along that complex path that will ultimately result in production and operational status. Since this process may take many years—and the ships, aircraft, and systems that make it will probably stay in service for many years—the character of Force 2021 may already be lurking on today's drawing boards.

There are two problems with this approach. For one thing, a lot of what is on today's drawing boards—probably most of it—will not make it all the way to the fleet. A survey of the drawing boards may afford a general sense of what could make up Force 2021, but it cannot identify which possibilities on those boards actually will be a part of the force three decades from now. The other problem is more subtle and more important: what is now on the drawing boards is rooted in the perspectives and concerns of the past. We are only now coming to grips with what the collapse of the Soviet Union means for the future and with what the military problems of the new era are going to be. As this realization grows, many of the ideas and assumptions that account for the preliminary sketches we find on today's drawing boards will become obviously wrong for the new era. A few years from now we may look back at the late 1980s and say to one another that a true historical discontinuity took place then, fundamentally outdating the embryonic decisions about future naval systems spawned before the Cold War ended. If this is true, it means the best forecast of the future lies not on today's drawing boards, but in what will be on the drawing boards a few years from now, when the notion of an historical discontinuity really begins to set in. What about extending today's ideas and innovations to their logical future conclusions? The difficulty inherent in using trends and ideas to forecast the future lies in separating those that will continue to evolve from those that will become extinct. Nevertheless, if we can come close to picking the ones that will survive, and think about how they are likely to evolve, we can build a forecast that will be as accurate as any other—perhaps more accurate. It is the approach I have chosen because I think it is a good way to understand the long-range implications of today's decisions.

THE PEACETIME PRESENCE–WAR-FIGHTING DUALITY

In discussing the future of naval operations, I suggested it was helpful to see carrier operations in terms of two general demands, overseas presence and war fighting, and that the mix of aircraft carried by the carriers could vary in meeting these two purposes. If we take this idea of dual requirements further, it may help illuminate the future.

One logical extension of the idea, for example, envisions a future carrier force split between some number of "presence" carriers—recognizable extensions of today's nuclear-powered carriers and big-deck amphibious ships—and very large, "war-fighting" carriers. Presence carriers could evolve from today's tendency to see big-deck amphibious ships as functional equivalents of the large aircraft carriers. Three decades from now that trend might culminate in the assumption that there really was little, if any, functional difference between the two platforms. We might think of both as multipurpose vessels, used in sea control and littoral warfare, strike and amphibious operations, important for the C3I and surveillance capabilities they carry, as well as for the advanced short-takeoff and vertical-landing (ASTOVL) aircraft that could operate from them. In both cases, it would be essentially the carrier, whether a CVN, CV(X), or the big-deck amphibious ship, that counted so far as presence missions were concerned. Flying a tailored mix of aircraft to these platforms in times of need, rather than having the platforms deploy with a standard air component, would be standard practice.

The "war-fighting" carriers, on the other hand, might be capable of supporting the operations of three hundred to five hundred advanced tactical aircraft as well as large transports and vertical-lift aircraft. They would be mobile sea bases, perhaps built from the experience and technology associated with offshore oil-drilling platforms. They would not move rapidly—perhaps we would build them by assembling components

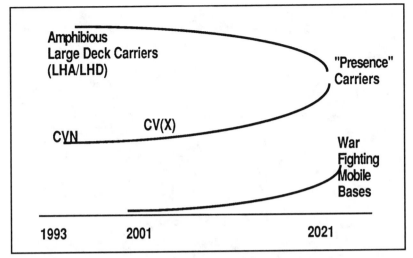

FIGURE 8:1 The Long-Term Future of Aircraft Carriers?

that arrive separately in the region of concern. Once assembled or deployed, however, they would be able to stay as long as necessary to resolve a conflict or to maintain U.S. military influence in an area over the long term. We could have an island anywhere we wanted one.

The idea of joining separate floating components into an artificial island has been around for some time. During World War II the U.S. Navy literally welded several logistics ships together to create a mobile logistics and maintenance base. The British built artificial islands in the English Channel to support the air defense of Great Britain. More recent experiments suggest we could assemble large sea platforms within two to three weeks. These would be deployable, albeit at relatively slow speeds (about six knots), and quite stable even in very high seas. Once assembled, these platforms could support the operations of large numbers of aircraft.[1]

The appeal of mobile sea bases is twofold. On the one hand, such strategic platforms could generate tactical aircraft sortie rates associated today only with large airfields ashore. On the other hand, it would be a relatively cost-effective way of generating massive tactical-air capability, compared to the costs of manning and maintaining the number of today's carriers needed to provide the same amount of combat output.[2] A force structure that included two or three of these mobile bases (one positioned in each of the hub deployment areas) could, therefore, turn out to be considerably less expensive and much more capable than one that did not. There is, at least theoretically, a trade-off between such plat-

FIGURE 8:2 Mobile Base of the Future? (Brown & Root, Inc.)

forms and today's carriers. For the sake of argument, a combination of one sea-mobile base and two presence carriers would provide much higher war-fighting capacity than five large carriers could today.

The concept of mobile sea bases would, of course, suggest three implications. While the U.S. Navy might have the responsibility of getting the components of the large platforms to an area of concern, assembling them into a large offshore operating base, and then defending and operating from them, there is no reason to assume that such bases would be exclusively naval. Indeed, the size of the assembled base and the length of the runway on them would be capable of handling any service's aircraft. The platforms, then, imply not only having a U.S. base in international waters virtually anywhere in the world, but also a breakdown of the traditional categorization of land- and sea-based aircraft. Carrier crews in 2021 might be very different, too. Reserve personnel might staff the mobile sea bases, at least until we need the bases for war operations. The aircraft using them might be reserve aircraft, or the approach could be to shift different mixes of aircraft from the active and reserve wings in the United States to the crisis, consolidating them on the mobile base.

TABLE 8:1 Notional Capacity of Aircraft Platforms

Category	Displacement	Aircraft	Current Platform of This Size
Small	30–40 ktons	40	Italy's *Garibaldi*
Large	80–110 ktons	80–100	U.S. *Kennedy*
Mobile Sea Base	>500 ktons	>300	National Airport

Some observers might see the mobile sea bases as symbolic of a U.S. rejection of coalition warfare, for they would erode the need for overseas base access. We could, I think, mute the image of unconstrained military power by associating the war-fighting carriers with reserves and using presence carriers in the ways suggested in chapter 2 to help build coalitions. The United States could assuage suspicions other nations might have about the unilateral capacity of the United States to wield its military power if we do not flaunt it.

Much remains to be said about the future of naval aviation. If the trends we see emerging today continue, two developments would turn out to be surprise-free regarding naval aviation. It would not be surprising, for example, if naval forces increasingly used missiles to strike a broader range of targets. Today, we can use missiles and piloted aircraft against many of the same kinds of targets, and as real-time targeting and sensor-fused submunitions come into the force, the notion that we should use longer-range missiles only against fixed targets will erode. More specifically, by 2021 naval forces may routinely target opposing ground forces in the field for missile attack. Piloted aircraft are, however, likely to remain superior to missiles in terms of close-air-support missions, or wherever there is the risk of hitting friendly forces.

Many of the improvements that will make missiles effective against mobile targets—real-time target acquisition, precise target location, and munitions accuracy—will also increase the precision, accuracy, and effectiveness of piloted aircraft. These improvements, coupled with a continued desire to keep human judgment in the loop where the lives of personnel are at risk, will continue to favor piloted aircraft in close-air-support missions. Because of this, while the applicability of missiles to the spectrum of targets is almost certain to expand, it would not be surprising if we optimized the piloted aircraft in Force 2021 for direct battlefield-support missions rather than for use against the fixed point targets that figure so heavily in strategic bombardment today.

The other surprise-free development in naval aviation would follow from concentrating piloted aircraft on close-air-support missions. As we move toward 2021, we will maintain the major difference between naval aviation and land-based tactical aircraft; naval aviation will be able to project power from the sea. The distinctions within naval aviation, however, will erode. I believe there will no longer be any meaningful distinction between Navy and Marine Corps aviation, even if there remains an administrative one. What exists a quarter century from now will probably be a single entity, rightfully known as naval aviation, and capable of operating from the sea and land as an integral part of joint air operations.

SURFACE WARFARE: THE TRANSITION TO LITTORAL-SUPREMACY SHIPS?

Suppose the problems of the littoral continued to dominate thinking about the use of naval forces over the next three decades. What would the effects of such a long-term focus be on the future of surface combatants? One could be the emergence of something called a littoral-supremacy ship. This would be a multipurpose vessel capable of performing many of the littoral-warfare tasks and functions we currently distribute among several different kinds of ships. Today, for example, we rely on Aegis-capable ships to provide air and missile defense. The command and control of a joint task force, however, would normally be conducted from another ship with the communications facilities better able to meet the C3I responsibilities for a joint task force. We normally assign amphibious-support responsibilities to still other platforms.

By the turn of the century we will almost certainly consolidate some of these various activities on specific platforms; we will, for example, routinely use big-deck amphibious ships as joint-task-force command nodes. A continuation of this trend, then, could culminate by 2021 in what I call

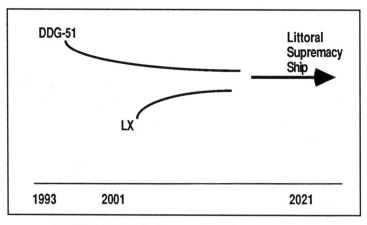

FIGURE 8:3 Evolution to a Littoral Supremacy Ship?

the littoral-supremacy ship. It might look like today's LX. It would blend the Aegis capabilities of an *Arleigh Burke* with C3I capabilities that go far beyond the upgrades we plan for large carriers in Force 2001. It might carry five hundred vertical-launch systems and new, high-rate-of-fire, long-range (sixty nautical miles or more) guns. The Navy might fill those vertical-launch systems with ballistic-missile interceptors, advanced TLAMs, ATACMS, or follow-on versions of such systems.

Such a platform could provide air and ballistic-missile defense across the littoral, joint-task-force C3I, strike and close air support, and direct and indirect fire support. With five to six hundred marines, twenty helicopters, and three or four air-cushioned landing craft (LCACs) (operating in multipurpose littoral missions from the mother ship), it would, as its name suggests, be a very strong asset, allowing the United States to dominate the littoral battle space from a single platform.

A multipurpose surface combatant could turn out to be a cost-effective alternative on a force-wide basis to a larger number of less capable ships. Savings would come from avoiding the duplication in electronic systems that currently raise the costs of new ships so dramatically, and from reduced personnel requirements. Such a ship would not be cheap, however, and as an expensive investment that creates something very valuable, the littoral-supremacy ship would pose two perennial problems:

—Would it be too valuable to risk in dangerous areas?
—What would we do with such a specialized ship if the Navy's mission shifted back to sea control?

Larger and more capable multipurpose platforms often raise questions about putting too many eggs in the same basket, and the hypothetical littoral-supremacy ship would, too. If we were willing to take the risk, and it was destroyed, would that in effect be a war-stopper?

It seems to me that whether the relative value of a littoral-warfare-supremacy ship would make commanders less willing to risk its use revolves around its vulnerability. The real question is the extent to which the littoral environment endangers such a platform. Today, we tend to equate the ability to dominate the littoral battle space with being there. We tend to assume, correctly so far as present technology is concerned, that littoral warfare requires the physical presence of ships relatively close to shore, and that because they have to be near shore, they will operate at greater risk.

The degree of risk in the littoral will be, of course, a function of how well we think we can protect against the dangers there. Today, we see the littoral as an especially dangerous arena for U.S. naval forces, a complex battle space where the weapons, communications, and surveillance systems we built for the open ocean do not work so well as we would like, and where the proximity of land reduces the time we have to react to threats. In the future, however, as our surveillance and information-processing capabilities improve, we may see these littoral conditions as much less dangerous.

The greater range and accuracy of our missiles, the growing ability of sensors to collect, process, and relay information about the littoral over greater and greater distances, the expanding coverage of ballistic-missile defenses are all positive indicators. They are technologies in which we could increase the U.S. lead by using the recapitalization strategy sketched earlier, which promises to give us the capability to dominate the littoral from greater and greater distances offshore. My answer to the question about the willingness to use an expensive, valuable asset in a dangerous area is that the commanders of such vessels would not hesitate to do so. They would not perceive the difficulties of the littoral environment the way we do today and would see less risk in littoral warfare.

What about the second issue? Will littoral warfare remain as central a focus over the next three decades as it is now, and if not, would a littoral-warfare-supremacy ship turn out to be like the coastal-defense Monitors the United States built after the Civil War, made obsolescent as the U.S. began to turn toward a blue-water navy and a more active global foreign policy? Would a littoral-supremacy ship be made obsolete by a shift thirty years from now back toward the problems of open-ocean warfare?

Several considerations bear on whether a concern with littoral warfare will last that long. It may not, of course, if a significant challenge to the capacity of the United States to use the seas arises in the interim, although it is difficult from today's perspective to see where this could come from. Nations have built blue-water navies in less than thirty years, and perhaps a challenge to U.S. dominance of the oceans in the future could come from threats other than navies (space-based systems or long-range aircraft, for example). The emergence of such threats, however, would in effect be a result of the inability of the United States to use its current superpower status to its long-term benefit. Right now it appears that the only way U.S. control of the seas could be ended would be through the emergence of another military superpower that wanted to challenge the United States for open-ocean dominance. Other nations, such as Japan or China, or supranational entities, like a politically unified Europe, will have the economic wherewithal to build the ships or other systems to do so. But they are likely to try only if we use our military power in the years ahead in ways that lead them to conclude that they must.

The particular issue here, however, is whether a littoral-warfare-

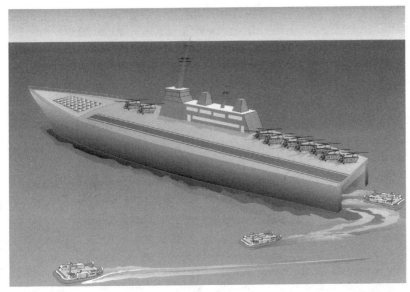

FIGURE 8:4 The Littoral Supremacy Ship, Circa 2021? (Lenora Sullivan)

supremacy ship could play an important role in a sea-control strategy, or would it become irrelevant because it could not adapt? I think the size and the multipurpose capabilities of this hypothetical littoral-warfare-supremacy ship would act as a form of insurance against irrelevance. The very characteristics that portend such power in the context of littoral warfare—the ship's size and multipurpose character—also tend to make it adaptable to whatever strategy we may eventually adopt three decades from now. Small ships are simply less adaptable to technological changes, and the best hedge against strategic change in the future is not larger numbers of cheaper, smaller, and more specialized ships, but the inherent adaptability of larger, only marginally more expensive, multipurpose ships (albeit at force levels 20 to 30 percent less than today's surface-combatant levels).

A Navy with three mobile sea bases, ten large carriers, eleven or twelve large-deck amphibious ships, one hundred littoral-supremacy warships, and forty-five SSNs—roughly two hundred ships, overall—would arguably be an extremely powerful, highly efficient, and less costly force.

SUBMARINES SPECIALIZING IN BATTLEFIELD SUPPORT

The discussion of future operations and Force 2001 also highlighted the capabilities of submarines to provide direct battlefield support. If we continue to emphasize direct battlefield support in submarine planning, what will it mean for the submarine component of force 2021?

One result could be the rise of modularity in submarine construction. The nuclear-propulsion systems of future U.S. submarines might be quite similar to what will exist in Force 2001. Nuclear propulsion seems most likely to remain the central concept in U.S. submarine propulsion as long as we want our submarines to be able to travel rapidly across long distances and remain undetected. Other forms of propulsion may provide equivalent underwater endurance and even greater quieting, but they do not appear capable of generating the power necessary for high-speed operations over great distances. As long as we include submarines in rapid-response expeditionary operations, we will continue to see nuclear propulsion as the most cost-effective solution.

To meet the kind of specialization I suggested was a logical result of a focus on battlefield support, a capability to attach a common propulsion system to specialized modules could become more important. Separate, specialized compartments could be built into a standard submarine hull during construction or attached to a standard submarine hull for particular missions; or—borrowing from the approach used with the space shuttle—the standard submarine hull could include a bay to carry particular capabilities, tailored to particular missions. This might include a special-forces-operations module, with bunking, messing, and other facilities for supporting a relatively large special-forces contingent—perhaps on the order of 150 personnel—for new forms of integrated special-forces operations ashore. It might also include modules that would provide relatively large numbers of unmanned underwater vehicles specialized for countermine warfare or other tasks, expanded communications and data-processing equipment, or what would amount to a fire-support module, perhaps housing fifty to one hundred launch tubes capable of deploying a family of standoff missiles.

The submarine will be an important instrument of littoral warfare in the future as long as there are no technological breakthroughs that compromise their stealth. Three decades is a long time for any assumptions to hold, especially ones that assume technology will not be able to overcome what we now see as very difficult problems. It is true, of course, that making the seas transparent is a particularly challenging task, but I think submarines will remain stealthy well into the next century not only because they operate in a medium that is basically opaque to most forms of electromagnetic energy, but also because they can adjust their operations and their own technologies to counteract advances in detection, location, tracking, and engagement. Neutralizing submarines is not a simple matter of finding a technological or engineering solution to a static problem. Submarines fight back with technology and engineering of their own.

THINKING ABOUT THE LONGER-TERM FUTURE

Speculating about the long-term future can help us avoid making incorrect size and structure decisions today. We should do it with imagination and a willingness to challenge basic assumptions. This is always hard to do, yet it is particularly important to try to do so now, when so much of the past seems inapplicable to the future. There are no proven techniques that tell us how to forecast the complex set of faiths and fears that will form the future political-military context within which our forces will operate, or to tell us what those forces ought to look like and be able to do. Yet if we fail to look ahead, the decisions we cannot avoid today will shape a mindless future.

Chapter 9

Some Conclusions

We were on a small Romanian ship going up the Danube. It was a father-son group—the Romanian Chief of Naval Operations and his son, a junior officer in the Romanian Navy, and I with my son, a midshipman at the Naval Academy. I caught the CNO's eye and experienced that instant, wordless communication that sometimes occurs. We knew that the next generation was going to be different from ours. And we knew that our navies were going to be in good hands.

I began this book by claiming it was going to focus on change. I would like to conclude it by returning to that focus.

THE NEW SECURITY ENVIRONMENT

The biggest change in the conditions challenging U.S. national security is, of course, the collapse of the Soviet Union, or, more precisely, the demise of the bipolar, superpower-confrontation world that existed while the Soviet Union was a viable threat to the United States. Russia still has the nuclear capability to destroy the United States, and the world we live in is volatile. Yet whatever history ultimately says about the remainder of this century, from today's perspective it seems clear that the fall of the Soviet Union began a qualitative new era in the international system. Much has been said about this new era, and certainly much remains to be said. It is hard, however, not to see today and the years ahead as very different from the past.

Different naval-force configurations are already under way. Joint military operations are moving to the center of naval doctrine, training, and planning. Littoral warfare is refocusing how the Navy thinks and acts. Quite simply, the nation's naval forces are beginning an episode of operational changes as great as any experienced in the twentieth century.

Major alterations in the size and structure of naval forces should be expected. To an outsider, the changes I sketched might appear to be incremental, for many of the ships, aircraft, and weapons systems that are now in or about to become part of the active inventory will be around a decade from now. Yet to insiders, the planned changes are dramatic. The number of Navy ships a decade from now will be lower than it ever has been since the end of World War II. The capabilities of the naval services, however, will be as high as they have ever been in the same period, and in some cases much higher. By the time Force 2001 emerges, the nation could be on its way to building a new Navy. That Navy, Force 2021, would be very different from what we see today.

THE BROADER PERSPECTIVE

It's only fair to put these arguments and suggestions into a broader perspective. They fit into a general intellectual framework I've been trying to construct as I've pursued the profession I chose some years ago. The first three decades of that pursuit happened to take place within a particular set of assumptions about threat and time. I wasn't the only one who worked from that set of assumptions. Virtually anyone who has thought about national security over the last four decades did so on the assumption, for example, that the future was going to be more dangerous. The basic national-security policy within which we worked—the policy of containment—actually contradicted that assumption because it argued explicitly that the Soviet Union would abandon its desire for military aggrandizement. Eventually. Yet until recently, what we knew about the Soviet Union indicated that that was not imminent. What we saw through the 1950s, 1960s, 1970s, and at least the first half of the 1980s was a growing military power in the east. True, Soviet military capability increased incrementally. But it seemed to keep going up, year after year. We debated the rate at which the Soviet Union was increasing its military capabilities and the character of those capabilities. We differed over whether the Soviets would use their capabilities, and if so, when and where. And we continually reviewed and assessed what we should do about it all. But we believed the trends would continue. And because of this, we believed the United States had to plan today for the kind of situation tomorrow portrayed by figure 9:1.

I think we dealt with the implications of this view well. The nation allocated resources—the trillions of dollars spent on national security—

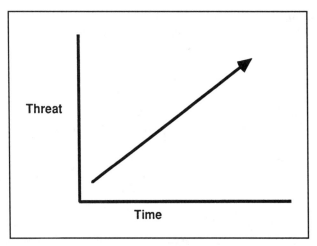

FIGURE 9:1 Cold War Assumption

in a balanced, reasonable manner. We spent what we as a nation thought necessary to deter war and to assure our survival if war broke out in the short run. We also spent what we thought necessary to cope with the greater danger in the longer-term future.

Because we worked within a vision of increasing danger for so long, it was hard to shift to another set of assumptions when the Soviet Union collapsed. So difficult, I think, that the current vision within which we think about national security is not too different from the intellectual framework of the last half century. Today's dominant vision looks like figure 9:2. It recognizes that the threat to the nation has declined. But like its predecessor, it also argues that we must prepare to eventually cope with a threat that will be more deadly, potent, and dangerous sometime in the future.

Why the threat will be greater in the future is not so easy to lay out as it was in the past. Then, we could point to empirical evidence that the military equipment produced by the Soviet Union was getting better. Now, the belief that the threat will increase in the future rests on long views of history or on dialectic assumptions that great powers inevitably generate opposing great powers, or even deeper philosophical assumptions about mankind's nature and the dynamics of human interaction. But whatever its rationale, I submit that this vision is now pervasive among those who think about national security.

This vision enforces a planning dynamic similar to what we accepted during the Cold War. It demands we divide defense budgets between immediate needs and the inevitable need to cope with a more dangerous

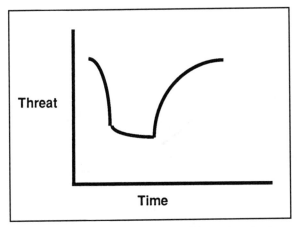

FIGURE 9:2 Dominant Post–Cold War Assumption

future world. Like the intellectual framework we left when the bipolar world ended, the new vision is deterministic. While the dynamic pushing toward a more dangerous future is unclear, this vision rejects the assumption that the world could become more benign over the long term. It says little about how we can shape a better future, instead telling us to prepare to deal with a worse one.

It is a vision that comes easily to those of us who have chosen a military profession. Because our profession deals with war, the most dangerous of human conditions, we do not like to underestimate threats. We tend to think about the worst things that could happen to be able to cope with them if they happen. We tilt in favor of the illustration above because we think that an inability to cope with a rising threat would be the most dangerous future.

Yet I think we should ask whether this view of the future, pervasive as it may be, is mistaken. It may be wrong because it denies our capacity to prevent the future it portrays from occurring, when, because of the collapse of the old era, we have more capacity to shape the future than at any time previously. And it may be wrong because if we believe it and plan accordingly, we may make it a self-fulfilling prophecy.

I think we ought to consider that the threat might decline in the future—and not rise again for some time. As a prediction of things to come, this assumption is as limited as any, but visions are more than predictions. They are also guides to decisions and actions. If we reject visions of a better world, we will act as if the world will be worse and cannot become better. As the world's only superpower, how we think and how we act has to shape the world. I say we ought to consider a

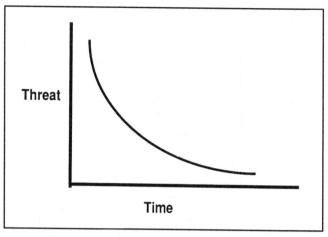

FIGURE 9:3 An Alternative Post–Cold War Assumption

vision of a better tomorrow not because the future it portrays is certain, but because we can make that future more likely if we try to do so. Figure 9.3 portrays this vision graphically.

This vision is not based on a theory of unilateral disarmament. I do not think the world would be a less dangerous place if the United States decided to disarm or dismantle its military-superpower status. On the contrary, I think we can bring this vision into reality with the help of our military forces, and that it is our military-superpower status that makes it possible to reify the vision.

We can increase the chances that the view of the future in the preceding illustration will occur by how we use our military strength and by the kind of military forces we build. We should try to do two things. We should design military forces, and use the ones we have, in ways that do not goad others to challenge us militarily, and we should build forces that are unchallengeable. These are the basic assumptions on which I founded most of the discussions in this book. They are the intellectual strata for my description of deterrence in the new era, the suggestions regarding the use of military force, and the ideas about overseas military presence. They help explain the case I have tried to make for investing in high-leverage military technologies.

I offer these views as contributions to the great debate on national security. Whether Americans recognize it or not, the decisions they make over the next several years regarding their military forces—what they do with the forces that exist and how they shape the forces of the future—will have as much to do with what the world will become and the posi-

Now, as I think back on my experiences with the Sixth Fleet, nothing strikes me more forcefully than the dedication of the men and women I served with during those fascinating years. Joe Mobley, carrier skipper, prisoner of war in Vietnam, was not selected for flag rank when he finished his tour, but he stayed on as my chief of staff and later returned with me to Washington as my executive assistant. When the Navy finally recognized his contributions and promoted him, my own service took on special meaning. He was pessimistic while the board was in session and assured me that he would continue to work just as hard no matter what happened. When he made it, I gave him one of my stars. The Navy is fortunate to have Joe Mobley.

R. D. Hohweiler, my flag writer, was as hard-working a senior chief petty officer as I have ever known. He met me on the quarterdeck every day, his work done perfectly, a professional to the core. After I had been there a couple of months, I asked R. D. where he lived on shore. He replied, "I live on the ship, Admiral. I don't have time to go ashore." The Navy is fortunate to have R. D. Hohweiler.

tion the United States has in that world as any other decisions they can make. My views will be controversial, but any other views about the subject raised would be controversial, too. Because of the times. In a new era, conventional wisdom is as controversial as anything else.

THE PASSAGE AHEAD

That is as it should be. No one can now predict the outcome of the great national debate on national security. Yet one thing is clear for the nation's naval forces: We have entered a rapid passage of events and changes. Not all the twists and turns, pools and rapids of that stream are discernible from today's vantage point, for it winds through uncharted areas. We know it will challenge the nation and those who have chosen to take the voyage. Changes always do.

The best way of coping with change will always rest with the imagination and perceptiveness of those who happen to be there when it occurs. There is no guarantee that imagination and perceptiveness will exist, and there are many reasons why they may not, particularly in the hierarchical, high-stakes institutions military establishments must always be. There are, however, some ways of increasing the chances that changes will be recognized and turned to the advantage of the United States.

One is to inculcate the idea that change is a constant. Uncharted passage is the environment of the future. We in the military must combine the value we attach to discipline and predictability with an appreciation that these important characteristics of the military profession are not there to inhibit questioning and innovation. We must be aware that we walk a narrow path between the dangers of mindless adherence to outmoded concepts and fashionable acceptance of change for the sake of changing.

We cannot forget that both of these extremes are dangerous, and we must always be as ready to question the validity of existing concepts as we are the validity of new ideas. We must raise these questions together. Specialization is a characteristic of military professionals in general and among Navy personnel in particular. It is the framework of the military organization. But specialization is not a justification for ignorance of the concepts and concerns of other specialists. To the extent we can develop dialogues across specialties we will create the kind of intellectual synergism that is needed to deal with a changing world.

What happened in the Navy between 1990 and 1994 shows that a large military institution can collectively develop a vision of its destiny and then move toward it. It all begins with accepting the concept of change, for ultimately, change is not so important as whether we recognize it, how we define it, and what we do about it.

Notes

PREFACE

1. Jonathan Schell, *The Fate of the Earth,* (New York: W. W. Norton, 1984).

CHAPTER 1

1. This is not to argue that all potential opponents of the United States will reason the way we would. As Desert Storm demonstrated, some opponents will not act "reasonably" even when confronted with superior military force. Yet while reason may not be the only factor that influences human decision making, it is likely to play some role in every decision, particularly in big ones like the difference between war and peace.
2. A statement widely attributed to a former Indian Army Chief of Staff, Lieutenant General Sundarji, when asked about the lessons of Desert Storm. *The New York Times,* 12 April 1991, reported his remark.
3. Statement of Secretary of Defense Les Aspin before the Senate Budget Committee, 19 February 1993.

CHAPTER 2

1. Saddam Hussein, Speech in Amman, Jordan, Foreign Broadcast Information Service, 27 February 1990. See also William B. Quandt, "The Middle East," *Foreign Affairs: America and the World 1990/91,* vol. 70, no. 1 (February 1992), pp. 49–69.
2. Secretary of State George Shultz, "The Ethics of Power," Speech delivered at Yeshiva University, New York, 9 December 1984.
3. Mao Tse-tung iterated the notion as early as 1938 ("Problems of War and Strategy," 6 November 1938), but the Chinese elevated the idea to dogma in the mid-1960s. See *Quotations from Chairman Mao Tse-tung,* Peking,

179

Foreign Languages Press, 1966, p. 61 (the ubiquitous "little red book" of the Cultural Revolution).
4. See, for example, Sir John Hackett's *The Third World War.* Although Hackett's book was a fictional account of how the East-West confrontation could spill over into armed conflict, it reflected many of the speculations within NATO during the late 1970s about how an actual war might begin.

CHAPTER 3

1. One of the best overviews is found in William J. Perry, "Desert Storm and Deterrence," *Foreign Affairs,* vol. 70, no. 4 (Fall 1991), pp. 66–82.

CHAPTER 5

1. The Army provides ample references. See, for example, Gen. Gordon R. Sullivan, "Moving into the 21st Century, America's Army and Modernization," *Military Review,* vol. LXXIII, no. 7 (July 1993), pp. 2–11.
2. See, for example, Lt. Gen. Buster C. Glosson, USAF, "The Impact of Precision Weapons on Air Combat Operations," *Air Power Journal,* vol. VII, no. 2 (Summer 1993), pp. 4.

CHAPTER 6

1. I think the definition provided by a fairly recent report by the Center for Strategic and International Studies captures the essence of the term's meaning. The report argues that the military technical revolution involves both technology and doctrine—technology (particularly with regard to surveillance, communications, command and control, and precision guidance) that allows the United States to "control a battle on a real time basis and down to an unprecedented level of precision," and military doctrine that is based on such capabilities. See Michael J. Mazarr and others, *The Military Technical Revolution: A Structural Framework.* Washington, D.C.: Center for Strategic and International Studies, 1993.

CHAPTER 7

1. Confirmation Hearings, Senate Armed Services Committee, 15 January 1993.

CHAPTER 8

1. Brown and Root concept, Taylor Laboratory OASIS concept.
2. During the Vietnam conflict the United States spent a considerable amount of money and time rotating and refurbishing the carriers it maintained off the Vietnamese coast. A large, mobile sea base would have been able to generate more sorties for less cost.

Index

About the Author

Adm. William A. Owens, the nation's second-highest-ranking military officer, is the Vice Chairman of the Joint Chiefs of Staff. His career includes numerous commands afloat and a variety of tours ashore with the Department of Defense, the Secretary of the Navy, and the Chief of Naval Operations. He commanded the U.S. Sixth Fleet and NATO's Naval Striking and Support Forces, Southern Europe, from November 1990 to July 1992. From July 1992 to December 1993 Admiral Owens directed the post–Cold War restructuring of the U.S. Navy, serving as the first Deputy Chief of Naval Operations for Resources, Warfare Requirements, and Assessments (N8). His early commands included Submarine Squadron FOUR and Submarine Group SIX. He served in four strategic-ballistic-missile submarines and three nuclear attack submarines, including tours as commanding officer of the USS *Sam Houston* and the USS *City of Corpus Christi*.

Admiral Owens is a 1962 graduate of the U.S. Naval Academy and holds a B.A. and M.A. in Politics, Philosophy, and Economics from Oxford University in England, and an M.A. in Management from The George Washington University, Washington, D.C.

The **Naval Institute Press** is the book-publishing arm of the U.S. Naval Institute, a private, nonprofit society for sea service professionals and others who share an interest in naval and maritime affairs. Established in 1873 at the U.S. Naval Academy in Annapolis, Maryland, where its offices remain, today the Naval Institute has more than 100,000 members worldwide.

Members of the Naval Institute receive the influential monthly magazine *Proceedings* and discounts on fine nautical prints, ship and aircraft photos, and subscriptions to the bimonthly *Naval History* magazine. They also have access to the transcripts of the Institute's Oral History Program and get discounted admission to any of the Institute-sponsored seminars offered around the country.

The Naval Institute's book-publishing program, begun in 1898 with basic guides to naval practices, has broadened its scope in recent years to include books of more general interest. Now the Naval Institute Press publishes more than seventy titles each year, ranging from how-to books on boating and navigation to battle histories, biographies, ship and aircraft guides, and novels. Institute members receive discounts on the Press's nearly 400 books in print.

Full-time students are eligible for special half-price membership rates. Life memberships are also available.

For a free catalog describing Naval Institute Press books currently available, and for further information about U.S. Naval Institute membership, please write to:

Membership & Communications Department
U.S. Naval Institute
118 Maryland Avenue
Annapolis, Maryland 21402-5035

Or call, toll-free, (800) 233-USNI.